POTENTIAL NOT PATHOLOGY

POTENTIAL NOT PATHOLOGY

Helping Your Clients Transform Using Ericksonian Psychotherapy

Paul J. Leslie

KARNAC

First published in 2014 by
Karnac Books Ltd
118 Finchley Road
London NW3 5HT

British Library Cataloguing in Publication Data

A C.I.P. for this book is available from the British Library

ISBN-13: 978-1-78220-140-3

Typeset by V Publishing Solutions Pvt Ltd., Chennai, India

www.karnacbooks.com

This book is dedicated to the memory of
Milton H. Erickson M.D., a man I never met but whose
influence on my life has been immeasurable

CONTENTS

ACKNOWLEDGEMENTS   ix

ABOUT THE AUTHOR   xi

INTRODUCTION   xiii

CHAPTER ONE
Developing the Erickson mindset   1

CHAPTER TWO
Utilisation   27

CHAPTER THREE
Altering patterns   45

CHAPTER FOUR
Multilevel communication   59

CHAPTER FIVE
The Renaissance man   87

CHAPTER SIX
The possessed boy who belched   103

REFERENCES   123

INDEX   127

ACKNOWLEDGEMENTS

I would like to acknowledge the inspiration, direction, and support of Bill O'Hanlon, whose encouragement helped get this book started.

I would like to thank Constance Govindin and Rod Tweedy of Karnac Books for their professionalism and willingness to help when needed. They made the publishing process easy and enjoyable.

I am so thankful to my parents, Paul and Sue Leslie, who have always been my greatest supporters.

Very special thanks to my beautiful wife, Dana DeHart, whose editorial insights, as well as her unwavering love, were the most crucial part of my completing this book.

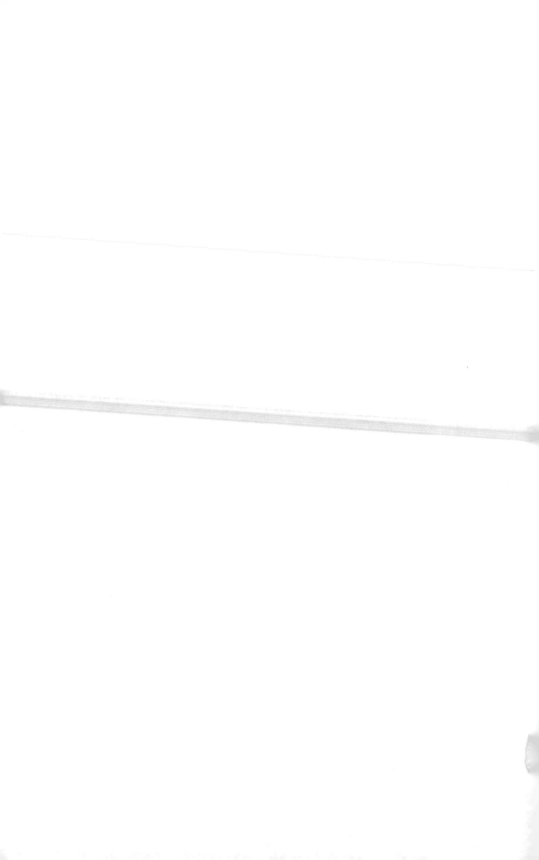

ABOUT THE AUTHOR

Paul J. Leslie is an author and psychotherapist in Aiken, South Carolina. He specialises in creative, resource-directed approaches to working with individuals and families. Paul is presently the coordinator of the behavioural sciences programme at Aiken Technical College. His website is www.drpaulleslie.com

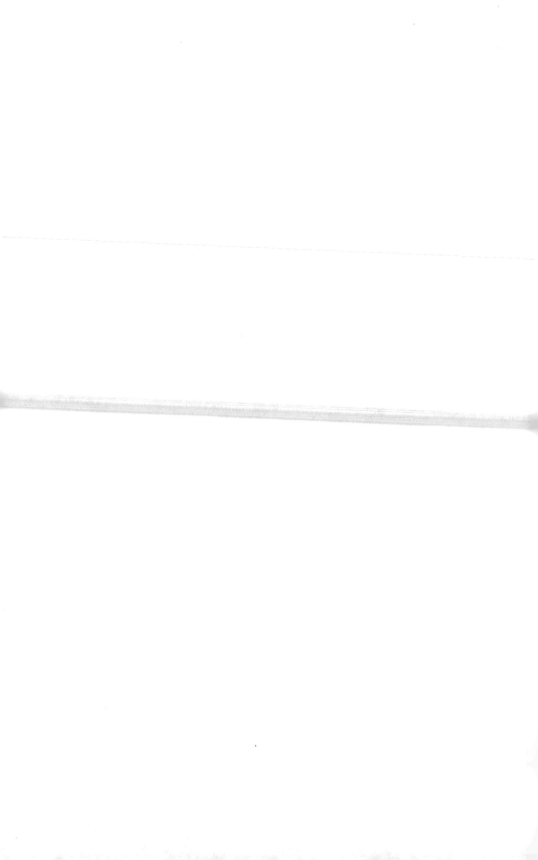

INTRODUCTION

Potential not Pathology is a short and simple book that is designed to assist therapists in re-evaluating and changing the way they work with their clients. I have attempted to make accessible to readers some of the basic concepts of Ericksonian psychotherapy in a non-technical format with minimal jargon. I found in my research that there was not as much information available as I would have liked about how Ericksonian psychotherapy can be performed. In this book, I am not advocating that anyone throws away his or her personal way of doing therapy, nor am I devaluing any other approaches to psychotherapy. I am not pushing anyone to become an "Ericksonian". I do not even consider myself a strict "Ericksonian" as I find that labels can be limiting (as Kierkegaard wrote, "Once you label me you negate me"). With this book, my goal is merely to introduce therapists to some unique ways of working with clients that they may not have previously tried.

Milton Erickson is a fascinating figure in the field of psychotherapy. His unique ability to indirectly create change in his clients has inspired many clinicians over the past 50 years. Some of his cases involving unorthodox and creative directives and unusual paradoxes have become legendary among counsellors. Erickson's work was centred in an inspiring belief that people had an innate potential to grow in spite of the enormous challenges they can sometimes face in life.

Erickson's influence has been substantial in the history of psychotherapy, as his work has inspired such areas as strategic family therapy, interactional therapies, neuro-linguistic programming, and brief solution-focused therapy. He has inspired two generations of therapists to move away from using long-term, problem-focused methods of working with clients and instead to embrace a brief, resource-oriented approach to helping clients change. That said, many people working in the counselling field today have never heard of him and among those that have, few incorporate the incredible concepts he devised into their work.

Milton Hyland Erickson was born in 1901 and grew up on a farm in Wisconsin. As he aged, he faced a growing number of trials and tribulations that required him to become resourceful and creative. It is possible these hardships aided in creating his positive, resource-driven outlook on psychotherapy. To begin with, Erickson was born colour-blind, dyslexic, and tone deaf. At the age of eighteen, he contracted polio and was given a dire prognosis. Erickson recounted overhearing the doctor tell his mother that Erickson would probably not make it through the night. Hearing the doctor give his mother this horrible news upset and angered Erickson so much that he vowed to live through the night (Short, Erickson, & Erickson-Klein, 2005).

He lapsed into a coma and several days later awoke to find that his body had become paralysed due to the polio. Not only could he not move but he also had massive difficulty speaking. Over the next couple of years, Erickson began to teach himself to walk again by closely observing his infant sister who was beginning to learn to walk. Due to having to sit still he began to hone his legendary observation skills and started to notice how his family communicated non-verbally.

During this time of self-rehabilitation, Erickson discovered that just by mentally focusing on the sensations associated with moving his body he was able to achieve surprising progress in obtaining the movement he desired (Short, Erickson, & Erickson-Klein, 2005). When he concentrated on retrieving memories of how body sensations felt he noticed that his body would respond in minor ways to his inner experiences. This discovery may have set in motion Erickson's belief in each individual having all the resources she needs to change within herself.

After Erickson began to regain some of his health, he started an intense journey of paddling a canoe down the Mississippi River from Milwaukee to St. Louis. He was supposed to go with a friend on this long trek but at the last minute, his friend was unable to go. Even though he was still recovering from polio, Erickson committed to undertaking the extensive trip, which lasted over six weeks, by himself. He believed this trip would aid in recovering his strength and stamina. While on his trip Erickson found unique ways to interact with people that facilitated his receiving assistance when needed. His diary during this time notes his wish to honestly earn what he desired but also be open to receiving help from others (Erickson & Keeney, 2006).

After his trip, Erickson found that his upper body had become very strong. He had made a remarkable recovery over the past year from extensive paralysis to walking with crutches (and even being able to eventually carry his canoe over his shoulder). With a couple more years of physical rehabilitation, Erickson became strong enough to attend the University of Wisconsin (Short, Erickson, & Erickson-Klein, 2005). His determination and perseverance set in motion a mindset that would also appear later in his insistence in never giving up on finding a way to assist clients in changing.

Erickson eventually completed college and then entered medical school. At the age of twenty-six he obtained his medical degree along with an MA in psychology. He became known as a psychiatrist with unique methods of working with patients. It was during his early years of working in mental hospitals with severe cases that Erickson honed his amazing skills. Some of his cases are well known yet they bear repeating as they give us insight into a different way of interacting with clients.

Erickson's way of interacting with and facilitating change in clients was simply unheard of during the time he started his work. It was truly groundbreaking because the prevailing view and practice of psycho-therapy during this era was based in a belief that therapy was often a long, in-depth process in which the client was directed in what to discuss by a therapist whose theoretical orientation placed emphasis on interpretation of client actions. Many in the field stated that it was primarily the client's insight into the presenting problem's etiology that would create real change. Through elaborate rituals based around tech-niques such as free association, dream analysis, and delving into client defence mechanisms, the therapist would dig deeper and deeper into the client's psyche until the hidden, unconscious motives for the client's emotions and behaviour would be exposed. According to proponents of these methods, when this occurred clients would be fully aware of why they felt and acted the way they did and to hopefully change their behaviour.

The approach that Erickson took was completely opposite to what passed as psychotherapy during this time. He felt he had more of a common-sense approach to working with clients than what he saw around him in the field. From Erickson's perspective, "it is a bit bizarre to put a phobic person on a couch and ask him or her to free associate for 50 minutes. It is common sense to get phobic people to violate their phobias by inserting them into the feared situation in such a way that they can learn mastery" (Zeig, 1985, p. 5).

Erickson did not believe real change would occur in a therapy setting if the only goal for the session was more information or interpretation directed by the therapist. He strongly believed it was the client's experience during the therapy session that created real change (Haley, 1993). It is only the experience of something different to what she is presently going through that activates the client's inner resources to solve her problems. Any extensive emphasis on the etiology of the presenting issue is keeping the client from accessing her natural abilities to heal, as more of the same bad experiences do nothing other than keep her trapped in the same place in which she began therapy. From Erickson's perspective, the idea that in order to heal, clients have to continue focusing only on their presenting problems, might even limit them in being able to activate their own ability to create new possibilities for growth (O'Hanlon, 1987).

Another fundamental characteristic that formed the basis of the way Erickson worked was his respect for the individuality of each of his clients. Because he saw each person he worked with as a unique individual, he never worked with any two clients in the same manner. Erickson did not feel the need to have his clients conform to any rigid theoretical model of therapy. He wanted each client to heal in the specific way that was best for her and not be forced into any preconceived patterns or techniques. Simply put, Erickson's approach was an indirect process of strategically assisting his clients in designing and achieving their own personal goals (Short, Erickson, & Erickson-Klein, 2005).

Erickson's interventions could range from outrageous to mysterious. He was able to get people to shift their behaviour and beliefs in unique and imaginative ways. Famed anthropologist and cyberneticist Gregory Bateson referred to Erickson as the "Mozart of psychotherapy" due to the incredible artistry of his interventions. Read the following two cases and reflect upon them as you go through the rest of the book. Notice how absurd Erickson's work can appear when one first reads it but when you understand the underlying principles that we will cover, you will realise how simple and effective but profound it can be.

Erickson worked with a businessman who had been admitted to the hospital due to his depression after he lost most of his money. This man would constantly cry and repeatedly move his hands side to side. Erickson noticed this hand motion and asked the man to begin moving his hands instead in an up and down motion. The man changed the motion of his hand movements. Erickson then took the man to an occupational therapist and had the therapist attach sandpaper to the man's hands. The man was then given a piece of wood to begin sanding using the constant up and down motion he was performing with his hands. Over time the man became more interested in the sanding motion he was performing. Later he began making various wooden objects and started them. He improved enough to be released and eventually made a fortune in real estate (Haley, 1973).

Louise was a violent woman who had been hospitalised due to her frequent acts of violence, including assaulting police officers. She was very aggressive in the hospital and would go into rages in which a great deal of damage to the hospital would occur. Erickson began interacting with Louise and appeared to have good rapport with her. One day Louise was intensely pacing the ward and behaving in a manner similar to how she acted before she had one of her destructive outbursts. When Erickson became aware of this, he signalled to the staff to begin destroying the surroundings in the ward. Louise was startled and shocked by what was happening and began begging the staff to stop. The staff totally ignored her and continued destroying things in a mad frenzy. After this incident, Louise never did any more damage to the hospital. She eventually began working in the hospital and was discharged (O'Hanlon, 1987).

With examples like this, it is easy to see why much of Erickson's work mystifies many mental health professionals who wish to emulate his incredible results. I have been studying Erickson for several years and I admit that I am still perplexed (and amazed) by some of the actions he took. I first learned about Erickson's work through my investigation of Neuro-Linguistic Programming (NLP). Erickson had been one of the main models that the developers of NLP had studied in creating their programme of study. The NLP developers mostly concentrated on the hypnotic language patterns that Erickson used. I learned a few valuable things in NLP but was more interested in the work of Erickson. The more I read about him, the more perplexed I became. I also noticed that most of the information about his work concerned his amazing hypnotherapy skills. I certainly wanted to learn all the Ericksonian hypnosis I could but I was also equally fascinated in his psychotherapeutic interventions.

I became so excited about the field of Ericksonian therapy and other related brief therapies that I found myself heading to graduate school to get a Master's degree and then a doctorate in psychology with an emphasis in counselling. Along the way, I learned as much as I could about all the various schools of therapy. I started my graduate school experience as someone who was leaning towards strategic family therapy, a style of brief therapy co-created by Jay Haley who was a student and collaborator of Erickson. I was determined to be a therapist who was creative and unique. I wanted to be more than just a traditional shrink; I wanted to be a healer. I wanted to be a therapist who could assist people in finding their own unique way to heal and psychologically grow. I desired to see the potential that each person brought to therapy and facilitate change using that potential. To say the least, I was excited about how I was going to help others.

My graduate school experiences, as well as my clinical supervision and field work, began to pull my attention away from focusing on the potential for growth a client brings to a therapy session. Instead, I was taught to focus on diagnosing "illness", medical model-based treatment planning, and a strict adherence to not doing anything that was not evidence based. Initially the things I was learning and doing perplexed me but eventually I found myself falling into line with the majority without realising what was happening. I had forgotten my "roots" in healing and had become a therapist who now valued interpretation, insight, and diagnosing over healing and change. I had begun to conform to a system that emphasised a focus on problems. I had stopped seeing potential and was now seeing pathology.

I began to find myself looking at therapy through the lens of what is wrong with the client rather than what possibilities for growth the client brought to her session. I began to see people as their diagnosis rather than a human being performing a certain action at a specific time ("The anxiety guy cancelled" or "Your 2 p.m. borderline is here"). I began to play psychological archaeology believing that it was always necessary for me to spend most of my time examining the client's history. Supervision sessions were spent looking at why clients were behaving the way they were and how to make them understand what they were doing. The therapy sessions I was conducting were beginning to feel lifeless. I know that clients did benefit from our work but it seemed to take much longer and could be hit and miss. I hated to hear from a client that things were no better after she had experienced a wonderful insight about her emotions or behaviour in our previous sessions.

Please don't misunderstand me—I truly believe that modern psychotherapy has much to offer people suffering from a variety of emotional challenges. But it often seemed that the desire to interpret client issues in the context of a problem, and the client as "ill", had returned in grand scale from the days of Freud. Worse, increasingly people were being diagnosed and labelled, and pushed towards unnecessary treatments and medications. I was seeing less focus on creativity and healing in therapy, and instead reading more on rigid, linear approaches to assisting clients. I did not want to admit it but, with some exceptions, counselling had reverted to the very thing that people like Erickson had worked hard to change.

Then one day I was brought face to face with a situation that shook me to the core and forced me to admit the state of psychotherapy was not as it should be when it comes to helping people heal. I received a call that a very close male relative of mine was experiencing a psychotic episode. From what I was told, I knew we had to get him help quickly. I thought about who and where to seek assistance but was stumped. The handful of therapists I knew that were good ethically could not see this relative due to a dual relationship with our family. I did not know who to send this person to or where to go.

The main reason I was so apprehensive was that deep down I knew that if my relative were to walk into most therapists' offices, he would have instantly been diagnosed with a disorder that would remain in his medical file for years. He would have been directed towards a psychiatrist who would prescribe medication that could be even more harmful to him than the episode he was having. I did not feel that what my relative was experiencing was something that required such harsh reactions from mental health professionals but I had seen how often medical model practitioners responded in such ways to similar cases.

During this time, I had horrible images in my mind of him seeing inflexible therapists whose only means of doing therapy was pushing him towards hospitalisation where inappropriate medications would be forced on him which would make his behaviour worse, solidifying his diagnosis as an unstable patient. I visualised the anguish of our family being told that he might never get better and he would have to be on medications and/or continue to stay at the hospital for the rest of his life. I imagined his health records being labelled with terms that would follow him long after his illness had departed. To be quite honest, due to my fear I was not overly excited about referring him to anyone. I felt trapped as I was afraid for him to see a professional and I was afraid for him not to see a professional.

Our family finally found a non-traditional professional in a town three hours away who did not diagnose and understood that my relative's behaviour was a temporary reaction to a major psychological event. Within a week or two, he returned to his old self and had worked through a good bit of his issue without medication or hospital stays. Words cannot express how relieved I was to know he was better. My relief changed to frustration when I realised that I had been afraid of sending my relative to my own profession.

Having to come face to face with the truth that much of counselling is based on problem-focused models of pathology, I wondered what had happened to the field I was so excited to become a part of years earlier. I was angry with my profession, which I had previously believed was a source of healing and change but now appeared to be more about insurance forms and diagnosing illness. This whole experience motivated me to change my perspective on how to help clients. This led me to rediscover the ideas and concepts of Dr Erickson.

I began reading (and re-reading) everything I could find on Erickson. With my perspective on the state of psychotherapy changed I now felt I was on a mission to find new ways of assisting my clients in finding their own individual ways to heal. I moved away from spending excessive time searching for the root causes of client issues and began to return to looking at what resources each person brought with them to therapy that could help them with moving forward in their lives.

I ceased diagnosing pathology in clients and set up my small practice; I did not accept insurance so I could avoid labelling.

Renewing my interest in Erickson's work gave me a shot in the arm of enthusiasm towards doing therapy. I found that my clients became more interesting to me and my results began to improve. This led to me writing this book about Erickson's psychotherapy. My goal is to provide fellow therapists with information that they can instantly use and indirectly rekindle their passion for performing the important work of psychotherapy.

Chapter One will cover how a practitioner can develop an Ericksonian mindset. We will cover how therapists can adopt a different manner of how to approach the counselling process. This will include how we can ensure we are approaching every client as a unique being; how to learn to become creatively flexible with clients (and ourselves); ways to adjust the focus in therapy from the context of client pathology to a focus more on the potential for transformation that each person has available to them; and how to move from a problem-focused direction to a resource-directed perspective.

Chapter Two gives simple explanations for the unique methods that Erickson used to alter behaviour patterns in his clients in order to enact change. The reader will be guided into viewing the problems clients bring to therapy not as a defect set in stone but rather as a process that can be altered with significant results.

Chapter Three examines the most important concept in performing Ericksonian therapy, utilisation. Utilisation is defined as using any behaviour the client performs as a way towards finding and developing a solution to the problem she brings to therapy. It is the practical use of what the client presents—emotions, behaviour, attitudes, etc.—in an indirect method of helping the client change. Also covered is how utilisation is applied in dealing with client resistance, acceptance of client behaviour, re-framing contexts, and the use of paradoxical interventions.

Chapter Four looks at the often-misunderstood concept of multilevel communication in Ericksonian therapy. We will consider what defines multilevel communication and the role of the client's unconscious in implementing this manner of communication in the therapy session. Also covered is Erickson's view on using the unconscious, and the creation and application of therapeutic metaphors and stories, with examples of how to construct healing stories for clients.

Finally, Chapters Five and Six present transcripts of therapy sessions in which the principles covered in the previous chapters are used. Along with the transcripts will be commentary about what is occurring in the sessions. All client identities discussed in the text have been changed to protect confidentiality.

I invite readers new to Erickson's work to approach this book with a sense of curiosity and playfulness, as nothing is written in stone. A good bit of Erickson's magic was in his ability to be open and flexible with an insatiable curiosity about what he was observing. If the reader has been previously exposed to Erickson's concepts, my hope is that this work will solidify and expand on earlier learning.

CHAPTER ONE

Developing the Erickson mindset

There are important beliefs and assumptions when working with clients from an Ericksonian perspective. Adopting these ideas does not mean you have to completely change how you work with clients. In fact, I believe that by adopting these ideas it will help you become more successful in working with clients no matter what your theoretical orientation may be. I recommend playing with this way of viewing therapy for a few weeks and then going back and noting how your sessions felt different. You may already be thinking in this direction. If so, wonderful! Keep it up. If not, then open your mind a little and try out this new mindset.

The mindset we bring to the therapeutic process may be the most important element in working with our clients. If we view performing therapy as something that is old and drab, we tend to get more old and drab clients. On the other hand, if we view therapy as an exciting journey of self-discovery (for both client and therapist) our sessions are often more animated and interactive. The beliefs we have as therapists may determine whether our clients improve.

I believe that therapy should be a life-changing experience. If a client comes to therapy and the therapist does not offer her anything different to what she is currently experiencing, then not only is therapy useless

1

but it is also a waste of money. I encourage you to make your sessions come alive with a sense of curiosity and spontaneity while giving the client the utmost respect and empathy. If it took something out of the ordinary to knock your clients off kilter then they may need something equally out of the ordinary to push them back onto the path of resourceful living.

One of the worst things you can be to your client is boring. I know that many of us are taught to be reserved and centred with no out of the ordinary behaviour while conducting therapy. This is to make our clients feel comfortable and safe. I think we can help our clients feel safe and comfortable while also being alive and interactive. Due to Erickson's belief that change occurs in psychotherapy not by the amount of information or interpretation given to the client but rather by the unique experience the client receives during his or her therapy session, his goal was to increase a client's chances for success, not to spend time on a never-ending exploration of where in the client's life she was inadequate (Haley, 1973).

Every client is unique

I believe the most fundamental characteristic of how Erickson worked with his clients was his respect for the individuality of each person. This meant he never worked with two clients in exactly the same way. Erickson did not feel the need to have clients conform to any specific theoretical model. By approaching therapy in this manner, he was able to create customised strategic methods of assisting clients in obtaining their own goals (Short, Erickson, & Erickson-Klein, 2005).

While we all think we approach each client as unique, the truth is that we often try to fit one client into the same intervention as other clients we have had with what we believe are similar issues. Sometimes this works and sometimes it doesn't. If we think of every case as unique we may discover more ways to help facilitate change than if we think of our client as more of the same. I have heard many therapists express either exasperation or frustration when they get a client who doesn't seem to change as quickly as the therapist thinks they should due to their experience with other clients who responded more positively to their standard interventions.

I once explained it this way to a colleague: imagine that you need your child to eat some vegetables. You are trying your best to get the child to eat broccoli because you like broccoli and the child's three siblings like broccoli. No matter what you do the child will not eat broccoli. You are in total disbelief because the siblings were open to eating broccoli and did not give you any problems with this vegetable. You try ordering the child to eat broccoli. You try to educate the child on how vegetables are good for people. You beg and plead with the child to eat broccoli. All these actions end in failure to get the child to eat this vegetable. Then one day you find out that your child loves turnip greens, mustard greens, cucumbers, and spinach. You now wonder why you have been wearing yourself out trying to get your child to eat a specific vegetable when this particular child was open to other nutritious green vegetables that you were not focused on.

Therapy can be a lot like that situation. Sometimes a person responds to your techniques and sometimes she doesn't. Thinking that the client should be behaving in the same manner as other clients is often unrealistic and will inhibit success in clinical work. Tailoring the session to each client not only helps the level of empathy and rapport but also increases our ability to find the unique manner each person needs in order to heal.

Erickson once worked with a young man who was unable to walk down, or cross, busy, crowded streets. Erickson figured out that his avoidance of public places was due to his fear of interacting with women. Instead of directly interpreting the young man's avoidance of these streets as a fear of women, or following the usual pattern of treatment based on what worked for other clients with anxiety issues, Erickson treated this client's case as unique. He focused his attention on helping the young man improve his physique. Erickson's encouragement in developing strength helped the young man begin to improve his body image. Once the client had more confidence about his physique, he began changing other areas of his life, such as moving out of his dysfunctional mother's home into his own apartment and being more open to walking down crowded streets. This was all accomplished without Erickson ever telling the young man what he felt was the real reason for his problem (Haley, 1973). If Erickson had treated the young man as just another anxiety or phobia case, in which the treatment was the same for every client, one wonders if such a shift in the young man's sense of self would have occurred.

When I was working as an intern in a community counselling centre, one of my first clients, Carol, came to therapy due to severe social anxiety. Carol had trouble talking on the phone to anyone she didn't know and she was panic-stricken when she had to go somewhere she had not previously gone. Interacting with other people made her so nervous that she would become disoriented and nauseous. Halfway through the first session I decided to myself that this was going to be an easy problem to fix. I was going to help Carol spot and change her irrational thoughts about herself and the world around her. I knew this to be effective way to conduct therapy because I had read, researched, and practised this approach in graduate school. I believed that as soon as she understood the logic of what I would teach her about thinking rationally she would instantly begin to change her behaviour and emotions.

Carol was a good client who listened to my interventions and tried really hard to do the things we had discussed. The problem was even though she knew her thoughts might be illogical or unrealistic she just couldn't seem to change how she felt. She would do her therapy homework and her relaxation exercises but she didn't seem to be getting better. She perfectly understood why she felt the way she did but seemed trapped in her present emotional prison.

This was a tremendous blow to my initial optimism about the case. I thought this therapy process would be easy. My worries were beginning to overtake me. I was beginning to become frightened that she would not be able to change and that this would be proof to the world that I was not cut out to be any kind of therapist. I wondered to myself if a good client like Carol could not change her thinking then what the heck was I going to do with someone who was in serious trouble or who was resistant? At this point in our work I wondered whose anxiety was worse, the client's or mine.

After a couple of sessions of this lack of progress, I reluctantly turned to my clinical supervisor, Jerry. He told me not to worry and to just keep doing what I had been doing. From that point Jerry sat in on our sessions and was my co-therapist. In the remaining therapy sessions, I continued to work with Carol on her beliefs about herself and her situation. Jerry, however, mostly teased and joked with Carol and me. He would listen quietly to what was being said and then say something that made us all smile. I couldn't see much evidence of any effective therapy going on from Jerry's behaviour.

After three more sessions with Jerry and me, Carol informed us that she had found a job. She further related that she had even struck up a conversation with a new co-worker. Neither of these were things she believed she could have done when she started therapy with me. She proudly announced that she did not think she needed to come back to therapy as she felt she was better. I was happy for Carol but totally confused. Why had she changed if Jerry wasn't working on her irrational thoughts? To me all he did was tell jokes and playfully tease us.

Before we ended our session and terminated our therapy, I directly asked Carol what had happened in therapy that had the greatest impact on her and enabled her to change. She thought for a moment and then replied with a smile, "I don't know. You guys are just funny. I laughed a lot." I then realised that it was not the information or insight that changed Carol, but rather it was the interaction with two strangers who made her laugh that was the greatest healer.

Her experience interacting with us in the office was what helped her become open to other interactions, not any techniques I had tried to impose on her. Jerry's playful teasing and jokes indirectly taught her that it was safe in the session and if it is safe *in* the session, it could be safe *outside* the session. I do believe that if he had come into the session and sat in quiet empathy Carol would not have learned to be brave. Instead of treating Carol as a unique client, I attempted to impose a technical prescription on her, which almost resulted in failure. From this I learned it is experience and interaction, not solely technique or insight, which creates change.

Becoming flexible

One of Erickson's unique qualities as a therapist was his ability to be as flexible as possible with each client. As we discussed earlier, if each client is unique then one's responses to each client will undoubtedly be different. In order to accomplish this, therapists need to be able to work in a seamless manner with what is given to them. Clients often seek therapy due to their perceived limited ability to cope with the inevitable changes that life can bring. Erickson has commented that the client's lack of flexibility is one of the most common issues one deals with in therapy (Zeig, 1980). I will add that it is also the therapist's lack of flexibility that is the most common issue one deals with in clinical supervision. If, as therapists, we are inflexible in how we respond to our clients this may make it harder for them to discover their own untapped resources and options.

Being flexible with client behaviour not only aids in maintaining rapport but also helps deal with frustration and burnout on the therapist's part. I remember a supervision meeting where Jan, a counsellor, was describing herself as "worn down" by one of her clients. The client would attempt to talk over her and he would instantly shut down any difference of opinion she put forth. Jan was attempting to be open and have unconditional positive regard for this client but it just was not working. She felt defeated and angry. All of us in the supervision group could relate to some aspects of Jan's plight as we had all encountered clients who tried our patience.

The clinical supervisor listened to Jan intently and acknowledged her distress. After thinking for a minute, the supervisor said that Jan might want to try being a little more flexible in how she responded to her client's behaviour. Jan was told that she had been playing the good therapist and being a polite person to someone who obviously had some communication differences. The supervisor suggested she begin each new idea with the phrase, "I know you aren't going to agree with any of this, but ..." and then give her direction or intervention.

The supervisor's advice worked like a charm. The client was so used to disagreeing with everyone that the supervisor knew he would disagree with anything Jan said. By beginning every intervention with Jan's assertion that the client was going to disagree with what she said, the client had to disagree with disagreeing! As a result the client began taking input and direction in a much easier way. If Jan had initially been a little more flexible in how she responded she may have been able to save herself some hassle.

In addition to being flexible with the emotions and behaviour of clients, it is also important for therapists to be flexible with their own emotions and behaviour. Erickson was very skilled at being exactly who he needed to be at any moment in his work. He could be the passive, loving grandfatherly figure that so many experienced. He could also be the tough, directive therapist who would take no crap from his clients. Consider this example of Erickson's persona in the following case.

A man was brought in by his wife to see Erickson. Due to having had a stroke the man was totally paralysed. He could understand everything being said but he could not move or talk. He had been in a hospital where some of the doctors had said he was a hopeless case. His stroke had kept him from his work, which caused his successful business to close. He was a proud Prussian man who felt angry and helpless at being unable to financially assist his family.

Erickson had been told earlier that this man was someone who wanted to be in control of every situation. The man's occasional grunts, signalling his exasperation at having to see Erickson and how long it was taking Erickson to write down all the information about the man's history, made Erickson aware that being in control was indeed hugely significant to the man. Erickson immediately told the man that treatment would not begin that day even if the man wanted the treatment. The man was so angry he refused to leave Erickson's office but Erickson had his sons carry the man outside. The next time the man came for his appointment Erickson told the man that a patient's job was to follow his directions without question. If the man refused to do that Erickson would end the session immediately and send the man away. Erickson told the man's wife that if he tried to communicate with her using any more grunts she was to tell him to shut up. At the end of the session the man was so angry that he ended up attempting to walk with his wife's assistance to their car.

In their next session, Erickson said many denigrating things about Prussians and scolded the man for being lazy for the past year. When Erickson told the man that he was going to have to come back to see Erickson and hear more bad things about himself, the man yelled out "No!" Erickson then berated him for not talking for the past year and how pathetic it was that all he could say was "no". The man kept repeating "no" and walked to the car mostly by himself.

The next time he came to see Erickson the man walked into the office with his wife's assistance. Erickson told the man that he was free to say "no" or "yes" to whatever was discussed. In addition to more insults, the man also began getting hypnosis work with Erickson. With Erickson's prodding the man began to start walking more frequently. He later regained most of his functioning and returned to his work. Erickson was flexible enough to use the man's anger as a motivation to begin healing his body (Haley, 1973).

When reading this example we need to ask ourselves if we can become as flexible and creative as Erickson in how we work. In order to assist a client in changing, the therapist may possibly have to be playful, unemotional, irritated, excited, or calm in the session. I have found that many therapists find a level of comfort in how they approach their clients, and refuse and resist doing anything differently because they have become too comfortable. This level of comfort may often result in a lack of flexibility in how one approaches a client. According to Keeney and Keeney, "practitioners who remain stuck in a particular therapy model or habit of relating to clients risk falling into a rigidity that prevents them from being flexible enough to effectively handle different kinds of clients" (2013, p. 123).

I have often heard absolutes about how one behaves in a therapy session. For example, never get angry in a session, never get sad in a session, or never show emotion in a session. I can understand how these absolutes arose and I believe there is some validity to those ideas but I also reject that one should always be set in emotional cement where all our feelings and behaviour are limited by opinions of certain perceived authorities. As long as we are not violating ethical rules and our actions are not hindering the course of therapy, why not be more flexible in how we respond?

Frequently, clients have gone through some kind of significant event that has knocked them off course with the direction of their lives. As previously stated, if it took a significant event to knock them off course, it may take a significant event to knock them back on course. If the process of therapy is not a unique, life-changing event for the client then one has to wonder why she is going in the first place. If we allow ourselves more flexibility in how we respond to clients we are in a better position to be able to make therapy a significant event.

In some cases therapists may have a fear of showing or experiencing their own emotions during their sessions. I think it is admirable that a therapist wishes to have control over his emotions. To me, being in control of one's emotions does not mean hiding or avoiding emotions but rather being able to access any particular emotion that is needed to help the client at that moment. If you find that you have problems tapping into and controlling the wide range of emotions you have, I recommend taking a few months of acting lessons. Learn to tap into the wonderful variety of emotions and actions that are available to us. When you are acting you can be anybody. You can be a hero, villain, femme fatale, a king, or a queen. You can play happy, sad, angry, or shy. Who knows, you may even learn to act in a way that helps your clients. They may come to believe you are a free-spirited, creative Ericksonian therapist even if you are not.

A colleague told me that he took close to a year of improvisational comedy courses. He then joined a small, professional improvisational comedy group in order to hone his ability to think quickly and change the frame of whatever happens in the moment. I could relate to what he was doing. Being flexible enough to see the humour in various situations has been something that has benefited me in my work. In many of my sessions with clients, we have been able to look at various aspects of what motivated them to come to therapy in a different way though humour. When I was once asked who my psychotherapy influences were, I included in my list Groucho Marx as his ability to see the absurdity in everything certainly coloured my outlook. I believe his influence has given me a much more flexible way of relating to clients.

Go for potential not pathology

In this era of psychotherapy it is all too common to find therapists spending too much time emphasising the diagnosing of illness or dysfunction in their clients without examining what potential clients can also bring with them. Many methods of psychotherapy used today mostly concentrate on pathology. What I mean by this is that the majority of the time the therapist will spend looking at what is "wrong" with the client and how to correct her psychological deficits. Due to having to work with insurance companies and various government programmes, the need to diagnose a client's behaviour and emotions as "illness" is often forced on therapists. This can set the frame of therapy as the treatment of a "sick" person.

Erickson's work shows a lack of focus on dysfunction. He believed that people had incredible resources to heal within themselves. He believed that it was the role of the therapist to assist clients in accessing their own natural resources for growth and change. The Ericksonian mindset is constantly seeking out the strengths that the client brings to her session. Erickson felt that clients often lose sight of their own ability to adapt to life's challenges and sometimes just need to be reminded of the resources they already possess.

As simple as this all sounds to do, many therapists have been taught to do the opposite. Many graduate programmes spend more time examining the client from a problem context than training new clinicians to find what positive attributes clients have that can be used in their journey towards healing. By being firmly locked into viewing psychotherapy in the context of a problem one feels limited in doing anything other than being drawn to the problem like moths to a flame.

Research in the field of neurobiology is now showing that it is experience that activates nerve cells, which then turns on genes that create structural changes in the brain, a process called neuroplasticity. This plasticity allows people to learn new ways of interacting with their environment due to the nerve cells changing their connections by either forming new patterns or strengthening ones that already exist. This is both good and bad news. The bad news is negative experiences can sometimes lead to changes in brain structure which makes the process of living rather challenging. The good news is if indeed it is experience that changes the brain then positive experiences can lead to alterations in a brain that was once structured in a less than resourceful manner (Siegel, 2012). "Vivid conscious experiences can turn on genes that code for proteins that lead to neurogenesis—the generation of new neurons and their connections in the brain. This new growth within the brain is the anatomical and molecular basis of our ever changing memory, learning and behaviour." (Rossi, 2002, p. 12)

So if it is true that experience shapes our clients' brains then we may wonder why so many therapists choose to spend their time working from a pathology perspective rather than a potential perspective. By spending more time examining the client's potential to heal and grow instead of constantly investigating the roots of her pathology, therapists can facilitate more positive experiences which may aid in creating new neural patterns for the client to gain access to life-enhancing thoughts and emotions.

When working with clients we may need to view the issue they bring us not as a pathological problem but rather as a process. By this I mean that a client is not an "anxiety disorder" or a "mood disorder" but instead does a specific process that creates an outcome that we label as a disorder. This process is a dynamic system of mental, emotional, and environmental interactions. Too often in mental health there is an "acceptance of a disease model without a focus on the intervening feed-back circuits that mediate the features of the disorder" (Porges, 2009, p. 31). By looking at what our client is doing rather than the label we assign to it we can have greater flexibility in designing more creative and effective interventions. This again requires us to focus on the potential of the client being able to change her process rather than continuous exploration of how dysfunctional the process is to her.

Here is an example. Tom comes to therapy and says he is depressed. He may have various reasons for being depressed but what we are interested in at the moment is the process he does in order to become depressed. We may ask Tom how he does depression, meaning what process he uses to feel the way he does that has been labelled depression. We write out a list of the actions he takes to get the result of being depressed:

- Think about the worst-case scenario
- Feel hopeless and apathetic about his place in the world
- Withdraw from others
- Sleep too much (or too little)
- Eat too much (or too little)
- Move his body very little.

At this point we have a blueprint of the process Tom uses to feel depressed. Instead of viewing his problem as a label we instead see how he continues to create and maintain this process. Rather than embark on an in-depth analysis of his past or immediately send him to seek medication, we can now work on implementing a new process for Tom to do. It might look something like this:

- Volunteer his time for a worthy cause where he can meet people and feel a sense of contribution
- Move for twenty minutes a day (walking, bike riding, etc.)
- Change the diet to food that provides energy and nutrients
- Adopt a more consistent sleep schedule.

Just by adjusting a few things Tom cannot continue to create the same kind of process he has been doing. This alone may not be a cure-all but it will go a long way towards showing Tom that he has the potential to respond to the world (or the particular situation he faces) in more ways than his presenting process. It could also give Tom a feeling of power to know that he is not a "sick" person who is only a victim of his brain chemicals or his past social interactions. Erickson's work with changing his clients' processes was genius in action. I believe he could not have created this genius if he only thought of behaviour as something stuck in a limited pathological model. A well-known example of Erickson's ability to embrace the potential within clients instead of their pathology is his brief work with the disabled aunt of one of his colleagues.

This particular colleague knew Erickson was going to Milwaukee to give a lecture and asked Erickson to look in on his aunt. This man's aunt had unfortunately gone through a series of health issues that had put her in a wheelchair. She lived alone in her inherited mansion with almost no contact with the outside world. She had curtailed all of her former social activities including the most important thing to her: regular attendance at her church. As a result of her isolation and disability she was experiencing depression and had even mentioned some things about suicide to her nephew.

Erickson agreed to look in on his colleague's aunt after his lecture. When Erickson arrived at her home she warmly welcomed him and gave him a tour of her large home. Erickson noticed how, other than adjustments made to the home to allow her to move around in her wheelchair, nothing much had changed in the home for many years. The house was dark and felt like a depressing place to live. At the end of the house tour the aunt was delighted to share her greenhouse nursery with Erickson.

Her nursery was a bright colourful area in which she had spent hours working on a variety of plants. He noticed the walls were lined with African violets, which she would take cuttings from and create new plants. Erickson complimented her on her propagation skill, as he knew it could be tricky to grow African violets from cuttings. The aunt seemed appreciative of Erickson's comments and it was obvious that this nursery was the only place she felt a sense of peace and contentment.

Erickson then began talking to the woman about why he had come to see her. He let her know that her nephew was worried about her. She understood and let Erickson know that she was indeed very depressed. Erickson then told her he did not think depression was the issue but rather the fact that she had fallen down in her Christian duties. The aunt was very surprised and offended by Erickson's comments. He said he noticed she was on her own with a great deal of time, money, and beautiful plants and she was wasting all those wonderful things by staying alone in her home. He directed her to obtain the weekly bulletin from her church and look for announcements of births, deaths, marriages, and anniversaries. Her handyman was to drive her to visit the people mentioned in those announcements carrying an African violet as a gift.

After some thought, the aunt agreed with Erickson's assessment of her not performing her duties as a Christian and pledged to follow his instructions. Many years later, after Erickson would tell this story to his students, he would share a newspaper with them in which the headline was "African violet queen of Milwaukee dies, mourned by thousands". In this inspiring case it is obvious that Erickson felt it was easier to grow the African violets part of her life (potential) rather than to weed out the depression (pathology) (Gordon & Meyers Anderson, 1981).

Focus on resources not on problems

Far too often we, as therapists, spend the majority of our time focusing on the problem the client brings us rather than on the natural strengths and resources each person has to work through problems. When we frame the therapy session in the context of a problem it can cause us to ignore or lose sight of various actions or emotional states our clients already possess that can assist the therapy process.

I define a resource as any emotion, event, belief, or behaviour that a client has experienced that can assist her in healing. If a therapist is working from a resource perspective he is constantly seeking what the client already possesses that can help move the client to positive outcomes in therapy. Often these experiences are in different contexts to what the client is presently experiencing. If a client is seeking therapy due to anxiety, then somewhere in her life she has also experienced being relaxed although in a different context.

As we cover the role of resources in therapy I would encourage you to avoid seeing the act of moving clients to a resource context as a technique. As Erickson often stated, each therapeutic intervention he performed was unique as the each client was unique. I invite you to think of these ideas as merely concepts and metaphors that may give you exciting additional ways to help clients. In Erickson's cases and in my own experience as a therapist, it never ceases to amaze me how one resource in an unexpected area can often lead to surprising shifts in a person's emotions and behaviour.

When a client presents a therapist with an issue, often the first thing many of us were taught to do is to look for the source of the problem by thoroughly examining the history of how it came to be, how it affects the client, categorising and diagnosing the problem, and deciding what actions we can take to help the client work through the problem. This is not always a bad formula but therapists often get stuck in a problem focus or problem-solving theme in therapy. When therapy becomes frozen in an investigation of the client's problem, the therapy process is then set in the context of "having a problem". Matters are made worse when the client begins to identify themselves as their problem. It not uncommon to hear clients introduce themselves as the disorder they have been given rather than other more enhancing aspects of their lives that contribute to their sense of identity. It is much easier to help someone who *has* a problem than someone who *is* a problem.

Being stuck in a problem mode of working can be difficult if one wants to rouse the necessary resources within the client to create therapeutic change. By centring the theme of the therapy session in the areas of pathology and dysfunction the focus moves away from gaining resources. This is not to say that we should not discuss the issue brought in by the client but rather that we might want to spend the majority of our time finding interesting and useful ways that the client can move out of "problem land".

Erickson was a master of helping clients access inner resources in unexpected ways. Consider these two cases involving clients with bedwetting issues as examples that show how indirect accessing of resources within the client can have dramatic effects.

Case 1

Erickson worked with a ten-year-old boy named Jimmy who had an issue with bed-wetting. Jimmy's parents had gone to extreme lengths to get him to stop wetting the bed. Some of the things they did to attempt to cure Jimmy was to have Jimmy confess to the congregation of his church about his bed wetting and wear a sign around his neck proclaiming that he was a bed wetter. None of this did any good and probably did much harm to Jimmy.

When Jimmy met with Erickson to work on the problem of bedwetting, Erickson did not even discuss the presenting problem. Instead he commented on Jimmy's athletic build and discussed what sports Jimmy was good at playing. One of Jimmy's favourite sports was baseball. Erickson continued to talk about the muscles necessary to play something like baseball and went into detail about the fine motor control that is required to catch and throw a ball. He spent time talking about which muscles of Jimmy's were most important in being able to close the glove after he caught a ball. Erickson then went on to discuss in depth how the muscle at the bottom of the stomach has the ability to stay closed until it is time for the food to come out. After three sessions Jimmy reported he had ceased wetting the bed (Haley, 1973; O'Hanlon & Hexum, 1990).

Here we see Erickson reminding his client about the resource that he already possessed. Jimmy was already successful at controlling his muscles. Erickson provided Jimmy with the resource for competence that resulted in his new ability to cease wetting his bed.

Case 2

A woman brought her twelve-year-old son to see Erickson due to the son's constant bed-wetting. Upon learning that the boy also had issues at school due to bad handwriting, Erickson gave the woman a prescription to follow. The woman was directed to wake up at four or five in the morning and check to see if her son had wet the bed. If he had not wet the bed she was directed to leave him alone and return to bed. If, however, he had wet the bed, the mother was directed to get the boy up from bed and have him copy out of a book to improve his handwriting until it was time to start the day. Over time the boy wet the bed less and began enjoying connections with other children more. He eventually ceased wetting the bed altogether and his grades improved (O'Hanlon & Hexum, 1990).

Again, Erickson supplies his client with a resource. He uses the boy gaining muscle control in one area as a means to greater control in other areas. By having the boy learn to control the muscles and coordination needed to write, the boy indirectly gains a resource that aids in controlling his body in the area of bed-wetting.

Dr Michael Yapko, a leading brief therapy practitioner, once related a case in which he watched his clinical supervisor work with a client who had trouble standing up for herself and setting boundaries. No matter what happened in her life she would not enforce her boundaries and say "no" to anyone. This was reaping havoc in her life. Yapko's supervisor realised that the client needed to have the experience of standing up for herself before she could use that resource in other areas of her life.

The supervisor began taking off his shoes and socks. He then threw them in her lap. The client was clearly uncomfortable with this action but said nothing. The supervisor then began to toss other items in the office on her lap until there was a pile of stuff on top of her. He continued throwing more and more items until the client, feeling overwhelmed by all the insane actions taken by her therapist, finally stood up and dumped the pile on the floor and declared that she was not going to let him keep dumping things on her. Her action of literally standing up for herself in the therapy session was a crucial step towards using that same resource in other situations in her life that she encountered (Kottler & Carlson, 2009).

A client I once worked with was dealing with her abandonment issues in adult relationships. Every time there was a disagreement within the relationship she would become angry and aggressive due to her past history of being emotionally and physically abandoned by parental figures at key moments in her developmental history. When an argument or disagreement happened in the relationship she would revert to her feelings and experiences from the past and act in less than resourceful ways.

It was apparent to me that she needed to have a feeling of certainty and security as a resource somewhere in her life to let her know at the unconscious level that ultimately she would be safe. Upon learning that she enjoyed camping and hiking in the woods, I encouraged her to seek some classes on outdoor survival in case she got lost while on one of her hikes. I warned her how dangerous it could be being left totally alone in the woods with no one to help her.

She agreed that it would be a good idea to know how to take care of herself in a situation such as being stranded in the wilderness. She signed up for an intensive four-day course that taught practical hands-on methods to survive in the wilderness with no tools. She completed the course and learned how to survive in extreme situations where she had no food, shelter, or water. After taking the course she reported a new feeling of confidence in knowing that no matter what happened to her she could survive even if she lost everything. In addition, she also reported that the intensity of her feelings tied to fear of abandonment had decreased. By having the experience of feeling safe and certain that she would survive in the wilderness, she could now unconsciously bring those same resources into the interpersonal relationship area of her life.

Helping clients find the inner resources to transcend their issues is an inspiring way to conduct therapy. Once you make the shift from looking at clients in a context of problems it will be hard to go back to doing therapy as usual. It is not anyone's fault if a therapist has been stuck in this limited method of working with clients, because this is what is usually taught to most graduate students embarking on a career in counselling. If all we know about performing therapy is based on problem investigation then that is what we naturally will do.

Even serious cases of behavioural dysfunction can benefit from a focus on client resources. Miriam came to therapy due to long bouts of depression and her cutting herself on her stomach. She cut in a very specific spot on her stomach so no one would see where she cut unless she was naked. This allowed her to continue her self-injury behaviour without her family or friends being aware of it. Upon hearing her describe her cutting procedure I was struck by how much consideration and time she put into cutting herself in a specific manner. I asked Miriam how she knew how to cut herself in just the right way to stay within the same small area of her body. She said she didn't know but she just did it.

I told her it was interesting that a part of her unconsciously knew just how to geometrically cut herself to avoid serious harm and avoid detection from others. I let her know that even though cutting herself was not a great idea to deal with emotional issues it did let me know that she was talented in the area of visual and spatial activities. This led to a discussion of her interest in art and design, which then led to a directive from me that she did more drawing and painting to satisfy the visual and spatial part of herself. Over time she steadily increased her artwork and steadily decreased cutting herself.

I have not always been so focused on client resources in my clinical work. I can clearly remember the day I was forced to realise that I had been lost in the land of doing "problem context" therapy. I had a very intelligent, nice client named Gina who had been suffering from the after-effects of sexual molestation she endured from the age of three to ten years old. Another therapist had diagnosed her with major depression and post-traumatic stress disorder. Her last therapist had even thought she might be bipolar. Gina reported that she would often snap at those close to her when she became angry and then ride the emotional rollercoaster, feeling guilty for her outburst. She was also tired and stressed due to having to take care of her mother who had been diagnosed with an undetermined neurological disorder. She had dropped out of college, where she was studying biological psychology, to ensure that her mother would be looked after in an appropriate manner.

I had felt we had worked well together. The usual focus of our sessions was on Gina allowing herself to feel her feelings about what happened to her in the past. However, she would return to the next session and report yet another episode of severe depression and anxiety including frequent sobbing at inopportune times. I was stumped on where to go in our sessions and was feeling incredibly ineffective as a counsellor. I cringed when she started yet another session by saying, "Well, I had another bad week again …" I was at a loss as to what to do in our session. I had listened as non-judgmentally as possible to her concerns and fears, I had compassionately challenged her dysfunctional thought patterns, I had suggested behavioural adjustments with systematic desensitisation, I had recommended mindfulness meditation for her to become non-attached to her emotions, and I had explored her family dynamics with ample time on the sexual trauma. At that point I thought I had done everything I knew how to do and I didn't like the fact that she was no better than the day we started working together.

All of a sudden something inside me thought about how I had continued to focus on her problem of constant depression and anxiety. Even though I was attempting solutions to her problem, the session was still rooted in the context of a problem. At that moment my mind was rapidly bringing to my awareness resources she had that could move our session out of the problem context. Gina had been successful in school in a tough biopsychology programme. She had an interest in yoga and the indigenous healing arts of other cultures. She deeply cared for her mother in spite of feeling burdened by her caretaker role. Before I realised it, I had asked her one question that surprised both of us and would change the course of our therapy session.

"Do you think you are a shaman?" I asked her. Gina was completely taken aback by my question (as was I). "Why do you ask me that?" she responded. "I don't know what motivated me to ask you but I notice some things that you have in common with a shaman. Shamans are known to be great healers. You have an interest in cross-cultural healing traditions and you have been studying how the brain works and how it can heal. Shamans can sometimes act terrifying and erratic and many people in their cultures fear but also revere them. You stated that your boyfriend and your family sometimes don't know how to deal with your mood swings but they marvel at how your presence is so helpful and healing to your mother. I am just wondering that maybe there may something to you being like a shaman. As I say this I know it sounds weird and maybe I'm wrong."

She sat still for a moment taking in what I had said. All of a sudden her eyes filled with wonder and tears. "Oh my god," she said. "I have never thought about it. I had read about shamans and many of them had to go through horrific ordeals before they became great healers. It was the ordeal that made them compassionate and centred on helping others. Maybe my past was there to push me onto a path of service to aid in the suffering of other people? I have always thought that there was some part of me that was supposed to do that but I thought I needed a sign to know that I was not so broken. This may be my sign." She went on to tell me that she had recently started reading the work of Carl Jung and was fascinated by the archetypes about which he had written. Gina related she had always wondered why her favourite movie had been "Return of the Jedi" until now as she now understood the message in it for her about accepting destiny and one's role in it. At that moment all the things that had happened to her were now strengths and markers on the path to becoming a healer and to be healed.

We worked on how she would deal with her emotions and actions from the perspective of a shaman in training. From that point on our sessions did not focus on how Gina was feeling that week or who had upset her but rather on the awesome responsibility that comes with being a "healer". Her challenges in life were part of a healer's path instead of a problem-laden existence of questioning why bad things had happened to her. Her pain was now her resource that could be called upon to assist her in her purpose and mission in life. She began to research further into the lives of other wounded healers who brought peace and comfort to their people. From then on her emotional wounds became gifts that allowed her to empathise with others she helped to heal.

Many of us in the clinical field may need to be reminded that our focus on the problem the client gives us will undoubtedly aid in maintaining that problem for our client (and the therapist) to "solve". As one of my mentors used to say, "You can never have enough of what you don't want."

Keeney points out that even to focus on seeking solutions is to keep the process of therapy stuck in the context of a focus on a problem:

> When we organize ourselves around problem talk, we get organized by the vicious cycle of re-indicating problem distinction. The same is true for solution talk, for it needs a problem to distinguish itself as a solution. Sometimes therapists assume they need to exaggerate the importance of a problem so it can be solved, resolved, admonished or exorcised. Whether you re-edit it, disorganise it, or

whatever, on one level, all of this activity is the same: giving the importance to the dramatic performance of a problem's absence or presence. (in Gibney, 2012, p. 69)

If therapists can move their focus away from the client's "problem" and towards examining any positive action, belief, or emotion on the part of the client as a signpost towards inner healing, then the field of psychotherapy could experience a tremendous positive shift.

Here is a case example:

> Erin, a young woman in her early twenties, presented for therapy due to the encouragement of her mother that she speak to someone concerning repression of her emotions. Erin stated that she was often the person who her family came to when they were angry and upset as she would listen to them and not outwardly be affected by their anger. When people did things to make Erin angry she would shut down and not acknowledge how she felt and would never address her anger with the offending party. The constant bottling up of her emotions was beginning to cause Erin some health issues in the form of acid reflux and irritable bowel syndrome. These issues are what motivated her mother to suggest Erin might need to talk to a professional. When asked what the motivation for swallowing her anger was, Erin replied that she was scared that she would lose her temper to the point that it would make life unpleasant (or worse) for her and her family. She was uncomfortable with any expression of anger, which was why she would work hard to calm people down in her home. At the same time she was growing tired of feeling caught in the middle of the many family battles that were taking place.

At this point many therapists would be either examining Erin's family history, challenging Erin's irrational belief that something terrible would happen if she showed anger, or invite Erin to feel the feelings she has been avoiding within the therapy session. All of these are valid interventions but are still rooted in the context of a problem to be solved. From a resource context Erin's behaviour has a positive intention. The positive intention I found in her swallowing her emotions is that she was trying to protect her family from her anger. Her desire to protect her family was then praised and cited as a resource she can use. Erin was instructed to make a nametag that she only wears at home that reads Anger Protection Specialist. She was told she should be proud of the fact that she has decided to care more about the problems of the family than her own emotional state. She is then sent home to begin her new "work" as Anger Protection Specialist.

At the next session, Erin informed me that she got so angry that she went into another room of her home and kicked a box. She was surprised that she showed any physical response to her feelings and admitted to feeling better after she kicked the box. She also reported that she was not wearing the nametag any more. I commented that it must be nice that she could stop being an Anger Protection Specialist when she wanted.

On her third session Erin reported that she was no longer feeling extremely stressed and her health had improved. She stated that her family had noticed a major shift in how she related to them and that she had also began to notice that she was occasionally getting angry but in "a good way". Erin was feeling more comfortable expressing her anger and sadness to her family and others. At this point she did not feel she needed to come back to therapy for this issue.

It is not uncommon to have trouble finding resources within our clients, particularly when they have been kicked around the block by life. Sometimes we may have to step back and double-check if our focus in truly on finding resources and not being drawn to problems. I remember in a supervision session a therapist was having trouble seeing any resources that her seventeen-year-old client, Antonio, may have had. Antonio had lost his sight when he was twelve years old. He was immediately put in a special school to help him learn how to navigate the world with his new challenge of blindness. Recently he was placed into a more mainstream school environment where it proved very difficult for him to adjust.

Antonio had been getting in trouble for fighting and his grades had slipped. Other boys would try to take things from him and tease him because he couldn't see. As a result of this he would challenge them and engage in fighting at school. Antonio's mother was very exasperated with him getting into trouble and would punish him, sometimes too severely, for his actions. His mother was an overbearing controlling person who one moment wanted him to become more independent and the next moment wanted to treat him as a baby who could do nothing on his own. At any moment Antonio would feel totally controlled and helpless or chastised for not being independent enough. Graduation was coming up soon but Antonio was not motivated to do the schoolwork in order to graduate and seemed to lack any desire to change anything in his life.

The therapist felt sorry for Antonio but was also frustrated with his lack of desire to contribute during his therapy session. When asked what resources he brought with him to cope and grow, the therapist did not know what to say as she thought about all the challenges Antonio faced. "He just feels so trapped by his blindness, his family and his school. I had hopes that he was going to be able to go off to college and get some freedom from his mother and grow up a little. Right now I don't know if that will happen. He is unmotivated to do anything with his life and he appears to me to be getting more and more depressed. He is talking less and less in session so I don't know if he has any resources at this point in his life."

After some thought I told her, "Think about it this way: Antonio chose to fight the boys who had taken his stuff. That is a resource." She gave me a very puzzled look and said, "Fighting as a resource? The reason he is in such trouble is that he is getting into fights!" "I know he is in trouble," I said, "but let's examine his actions from a different perspective. Antonio is fighting because he is standing up for himself. Isn't that what we as adults are taught to do? He cares enough about himself that he will not, even as a blind child, allow anyone to steal from him or push him around. There are many kids who have their sight who won't stand up for themselves. I know violence is not a solution but his desire to stand up for himself is a great resource that he can use in other areas of his life."

She thought about it and then we began brainstorming ways that Antonio can stand up for other things in his life the way he stood up against the boys who were bullying him. She decided that Antonio should be praised for not letting people bully him. Although she would let him know that violence is not always a good option for dealing with conflict, she would boast about him in their session for being strong enough to not back down to the boys bullying him. She would let him know that his actions showed he had courage and strength. This was also the first time in a long time that anyone had boasted about Antonio. This increased the rapport between Antonio and the therapist and also gave her a new positive direction for their future sessions.

Results not reasons

Looking for the cause or reasons for a certain behaviour is very common in most traditional therapies. It is still a common belief among therapists that it is very important that a client have a full understanding and insight into why they do, act, or feel a certain way. I believe this is a holdover from the psychodynamic era in which Freud and many of his followers thought that the goal of therapy was for the client to fully comprehend the reasons for their issue. In order to get to this point, therapists had to look intently at the dark areas of the client's life to discover how the dysfunction started. I call this approach "psychological archaeology".

If we operate with an Ericksonian mindset, we realise that the past does contain elements that may have helped shape the client's present reality; however, change is not rooted in constant exploration of the past. Endless speculation and exploration of one's past often yields little to no results in moving a client in a new direction in life. By the time many clients come to therapy they have already speculated and explored why the present situation they are in has happened. It is not uncommon for many therapists to have clients who know all the reasons for the way they are but they have no real plan as to how to change. Knowing why a person started smoking has little to no impact on her ability to stop. Knowing why a person has boundary issues may be nice for the client to understand where the problem originated but it does nothing to change the behaviour that continues to create the problem.

In many cases it is not essential to gain all the historical facts about how the situation developed. Often even just a little bit of information is all that is needed for the therapist to begin assisting clients in changing their present situations. Viewing therapy from this perspective, I advocate the maxim "less is more". Get the information that is needed but not more than is necessary. We need to cease our compulsion to do psychological archaeology and instead deal with what we need to do to move the client forward. We can't do that very well if our entire focus is on finding and spending long periods in those dark historical causes for the problem. Insight about the reasons for present behaviour is not necessary to change that behaviour. The continued need to understand the motivations for why a client behaves in a certain way may also further the client's identification with the very problem for which she seeks help.

I once had a client, Lily, who had come to therapy to deal with her anxiety. She seemed to have trouble getting comfortable in most situations and appeared to be unable to sit still for any period of time. After talking with her for a while she wanted to tell me about the first time she said she felt really scared in a big way. Lily was rather hesitant in getting out this information so I assured her that no matter what, she would not be judged harshly for what she had done or experienced. She finally spoke up and said that when she was eight years old her family moved into a "haunted house".

This immediately got my attention because I was not expecting this kind of story at all. Lily further stated that no one in her family believed in ghosts until they moved into this particular home. She gave me several examples of weird, scary things that happened in the home. After relating some spooky incidents, she then told me about a specific time she was truly terrified. She was in her room one day and looked up and saw a ghostly apparition of a young girl. She felt a mixture of adrenaline-dumping fear and an overwhelming sadness. Lily jumped up and ran as fast as she could to get out of the room. She told me she never went in her bedroom again. Her family eventually moved out of the house but from that point Lily had become an anxious child who turned into an anxious adult.

After hearing this story and seeing how certain Lily was that this was her main issue, I decided to design a therapeutic intervention based around her experience of being afraid of this ghost. After a short time of our work on this issue Lily had become more relaxed and stated that she now was able to sleep better as she was not so afraid of spectral phenomena. She appeared less apprehensive about life in general and even took the risk of changing jobs to follow her long-term dreams.

I was very happy with the way this case had gone (and the novelty of ghosts being involved was so cool) so I presented this particular case in a supervision session. After relating the story of Lily's haunted adventures and how we had worked to have a major decrease in her anxiety, I was immediately told that I needed to be more careful in working with this woman. I was informed that there must have been something else in her past that was causing her anxiety. In addition I was politely reminded that seeing ghosts is sometimes a way people deal with sexual abuse and it would have been a good idea to find out more about Lily's relationship with her father.

I was astounded by what I was hearing. I had come to this supervision session expecting a very different response. From my perspective I had related that Lily's anxiety was much better and she was happier. I thought that the great result with Lily was the most important thing to discuss, not the need to explore those dark, deep layers of the psyche. My colleagues were more interested in finding out any other terrible reasons she had for being anxious rather than the positive result we had obtained. I could understand digging further if maybe Lily's condition had not improved but she had improved in a major way. This point seemed to escape my well-meaning colleagues.

In essence, we need to focus on the results of our therapy sessions and not on the reasons the client is the way she is. I believe in honouring the past but not getting stuck in it. Often your client is stuck in the past in some way and having you there with her isn't going to get her to move towards a life-enhancing future. We need to be future oriented in our interventions, not past centred. Talking about the past and honouring the person's previous experience is fine but if the therapist spends the majority of his time discussing past hurts then little time is left for creating new possibilities for the client to experience.

This point was driven home by my friend William Oliver who shared with me a remarkably effective form of regression therapy in which the therapist regresses the client rapidly back to the first time a specific negative event happened, releases any old emotional wounds, and then builds a new way of responding to the old situation. This approach usually takes no more than two sessions. I was commenting on how this form of therapy has to go back to the past first before assisting the client in building a new future. I told him that this type of therapy seemed a little bit similar to some other therapies that regress and use the client's past history. He replied: "Possibly but this method is taking the client back to the past for a very, very short time and then it is over. After that one time the therapist never goes back to the past but instead moves the client forward towards building a new way of being in the world where the past is no longer the thing blocking the client. Why would anyone want to keep going back to the traumatic past session after session? Wasn't it bad enough the first time?"

* * *

By opening their minds to these concepts I believe therapists will become more dynamic and effective professionals and will find the therapeutic process becomes more alive and productive. Imagine sitting with a new client and noticing more of what is possible for her rather than what is not working. Just by shifting our mindset in this direction we can accomplish so much more in our work. Instead of seeing each person as a possessor of a mental "disease", a history of pathology, or the latest guinea pig on which to try out the same evidence-based technique over and over again, why not make therapy an exciting, improvisational experience that creates surprising results? Isn't that really why we all got started in the field?

CHAPTER TWO

Utilisation

The most important concept for anyone interested in working from an Ericksonian perspective is utilisation. The main reason Erickson was so effective in his work was his abundant use of utilisation. Stephen Gilligan, one of Erickson's direct students and the creator of self-relations psychotherapy, has remarked that utilisation is probably Erickson's most important contribution to the field of therapy (2002).

Whereas many therapists have predetermined patterns and techniques for their clients, Ericksonian therapists often appear to have no specific agenda. No matter what the client presented in the session, Erickson believed in using any experiences or actions presented by the client to facilitate growth. Utilisation is the creative process of integrating aspects of client behaviour and attitude into a method for developing therapeutic change. Utilisation can be seen as "a perspective of optimism and confidence in the clients' ability to respond to treatment" (Dolan, 1985, p. 7). Erickson saw any and every action of his client as helpful in assisting the client to access more of their own personal resources to make different and empowering choices for themselves.

Therapists often have certain requisites for how their clients need to act or feel in order for therapy to be successful. Erickson did not

27

appear to have any set precondition for his clients, even when they presented incredibly dysfunctional behaviour. What is remarkable about Erickson's approach was not only did he see to it that these behaviours didn't obstruct the therapy process, but he was also able to use these same dysfunctional behaviours to advance the achievement of the therapeutic outcome.

Rather than fighting his client's resistant actions, Erickson would use what other therapists would see as defensive resistance as a way of moving clients towards the solution to their problems. "Instead of attributing unworkability to rigid personality characteristics, Erickson would take it upon himself to learn the individual's pattern of behaviour and response. He would then utilise these patterns in service of change, rather than treating them as blocks." (O'Hanlon, 1987, p. 10) Erickson accepted his client's right to behave in a resistant manner and arranged situations so that in order to resist the therapist, the client had to respond in a way that is constructive to the therapy process.

When the resistance is openly acknowledged and encouraged, it can then be directed towards assisting the therapy rather than hindering it. Even the symptoms the client brings to therapy can be utilised towards achieving healing. The Ericksonian perspective is that "anything that occurs in the therapy session can be used to initiate therapeutic movement, be it resistance, anger or a preferred topic of conversation, a behaviour, or even an error on the part of the therapist" (Havens, 1996, p. 205). It makes no difference what happens in the session, as the therapist operating from an Ericksonian perspective will use it for change. By maintaining a non-judgmental attitude towards the resistance, the therapist allows for the possibility of the client's resistance to become a beneficial resource that can facilitate and enhance the therapeutic process.

Erickson stated, "When you understand how man really defends his intellectual ideas and how emotional he gets about it, you should realise that the first thing in psychotherapy is not to try to compel his ideation; rather, you go along with it and change it in a gradual fashion and create situations wherein he himself willingly changes his thinking" (Erickson & Zeig, 1980, p. 335). To be successful at utilisation the therapist needs to acquire an intense focus on the client's beliefs about why she is in therapy and what is needed to change. Utilising the beliefs the client brings to her session aids in building a strong therapeutic alliance that will allow both therapist and client to work collaboratively in resolving the client's problem.

Simply put, utilisation is the acceptance and validation of any behaviour, thought, or emotion that a client exhibits as a foundation for creating a desired therapeutic outcome. By accepting the client's experiences, even when dysfunctional and limited, the therapist is able to build a relationship with the client in a manner that allows the therapist to channel the client's experiences in the direction of a more resourceful way of being in the world. When the therapist cooperates with the unconscious patterns the client presents and adjusts his therapeutic approach to what is happening with the client in the moment, this can create an opening for the therapist to indirectly move the client towards more useful resources. The inclusion and validation of the client's experiences is a key to moving forward with interventions to widen the client's perspective of what is possible for them. Dr Jeffrey Zeig, a long-time student of Erickson, once stated in a seminar that utilisation is essentially asking how we can find virtue in our faults.

Often we find the client has relinquished all her power to the problem that causes suffering. In many instances the client has even come to identify her sense of self with the problem. When this happens resistance is inevitably encountered, as any change in the problem creates a need for change in the client's identity, which for most people is scary. People often choose to maintain even the most dysfunctional behaviour rather than reformulate their sense of self. I have even heard a client ask, "Who would I be without my problem?" In these situations it is imperative the therapist offers acceptance of the problem as this may be the only way to obtain any adjustment of the client's situation. Utilisation gives the therapist the ability to transform the client's relationship to the problem without directly forcing her to change her sense of self.

A great example of Erickson's gifted use of utilisation is an often-cited case in which he worked with a suicidal woman. This young woman came to see Erickson because she had lost any sense of hope in her life. Her parents had died as a result of a car crash in the recent past and she felt no sense of connection with others. She related to Erickson that she felt her life was aimless and she was never satisfied with it. She also related to him that she felt herself to be ugly. This was mostly due to a small gap between her two front teeth. She told Erickson she believed the gap between her teeth seemed to be an insurmountable obstacle for her in finding a husband and having a family. She felt so ugly that she attempted to hide her face as often as possible. Erickson noticed she took little care in her appearance as her clothes were worn and unmatched and her overall appearance was sloppy.

Since she felt her life had no meaning to her she told Erickson she had decided to commit suicide in three months. She let Erickson know that her mind was made up and not much he could say would keep her from carrying out the task. Upon questioning her about other areas of her life Erickson learned there was a young man at work who seemed to be interested in her. The young woman also appeared to be interested in him but her fear about her appearance kept her at a distance although the two of them often seemed to find a way to be at the water fountain at the same time.

Erickson told the young woman that indeed there was little he could do to stop her in three months. He then told her that since she was not going to be around in a few months she might was well live it up and treat herself to some fun. He directed her to take her savings in the bank and go shopping for new clothes. He also told her to go to the hairdresser and get a new hairstyle. Somehow Erickson also got the woman to begin practicing squirting water through the gap in her front teeth. When she became proficient at squirting water through her teeth, Erickson convinced her to use this new skill to play a practical joke on the young man at the water fountain at work by squirting him with water after she had a drink from the cooler. Erickson directed her to dress up in her best new clothes and meet the young man at the fountain. She was then to squirt him with water and run away as fast as she could.

When the woman returned to her next session she related to Erickson that she had followed his instructions. She told him the young man was surprised when she sprayed him with water and chased after her when she ran away. He caught her and had kissed her. After this incident, the two began dating. Several months later she did not commit suicide but instead married the young man she had squirted with water. A year later Erickson was informed she was having her first child (O'Hanlon & Hexum, 1990).

In this classic case, Erickson fully avoided any direct confrontation of the young woman's decision to end her life in three months. He wisely saw that attempting to coerce the client to abandon her decision was doomed to fail. Instead he used the very thing she was most ashamed of, the gap in her front teeth, as a resource for creating a life-changing experience for her.

I once heard about a male therapist who had a female client who came to see him due to her issues with alcohol use. The client was financially supported by her overbearing but extremely distant father, who was very wealthy. All the client did was go shopping, attend parties, and hang out with other wealthy people who were also miserable and addicted to alcohol. She lived in an emptiness that was only bearable due to her lavish lifestyle and Daddy's ability to pick up the bill for all of it, including her short stays at rehabilitation centres. She desperately wanted her father's approval but the only way her father had ever known how interact with his daughter was to throw money at whatever she wanted and then go back to his world of financial conquest. She had lost her mother in a tragic accident when she was very young and as a result her world was centred on her father.

Early in their session, the therapist noticed how much the client playfully flirted with him. He recognised that this behaviour was how she had been able to connect and control the people in her life (particularly her father). Instead of challenging her on her flirting he chose to utilise it as a resource. He directly told her that he noticed she was flirting with him and that he thought she was excellent at it. She was surprised and almost a little offended that she was found out. He countered with a long discussion about what a gift her flirting was, as so many women don't know how to flirt. He told her that many women will come on to men way too strong or will act submissive or weak when they flirt but she, on the other hand, was a master at knowing how to flirt in a wonderfully respectful way. He recommended that she give serious thought to teaching other women how to flirt effectively. He told her that there were probably many professional women who were so work focused that they had either forgotten how to flirt or perhaps never learned to do it. Since flirting requires no formal education or training he suggested she consider starting a small class for women only. The client was intrigued by this idea.

Over the next few months, the client did indeed start a small class, for professional women only, on the fine art of flirting. She found out that she was a natural teacher and what she had to present was warmly received by her students. As she taught her classes she began to experience the feelings of appreciation and acceptance from the women she was teaching. She was surprised that these professional women were really interested in what she had to say. As time went on she began decreasing her drinking while connecting more with other women, of whom many were interested in assisting her grow her new business. She began to rely less and less on her father as her self-confidence grew. If the therapist had not utilised the woman's flirtatious behaviour in a positive manner, the positive outcome of her therapy may not have developed.

In one of Erickson's most celebrated cases, he worked with a hospital patient who believed he was Jesus Christ. This man created disturbances on the ward due to his aggressive preaching and proselytising. Erickson simply approached the man and asked if he was indeed Jesus Christ. The man replied he was. Erickson then told the man that since he was Jesus, he knew the man had been a carpenter. The man replied he had indeed been a carpenter. Erickson then asked the man for his help with building a bookcase. The man agreed, which began the process of moving him towards more productive work and positive interactions with others (Haley, 1973).

I read recently of a great example of utilisation by the staff of a nursing home. A patient was consistently attempting to leave the home to get to the bus stop in order to go home. This patient had no relatives near her and her home had been sold several years previously. She was suffering from the early stages of Alzheimer's disease and would sometimes get quite confused about where she was. The only logical solution in her mind was to take the bus home.

Unfortunately for her, there was no bus stop near the home. When she went outside she would see there was no bus stop and then wander away to attempt to find one. This often put her in great danger as she was already confused due to her illness and the home was in a very congested and busy part of the city. If a staff member tried to get her to come inside she would often attempt to run away from them and become very obstinate about going back.

After the staff realised her attempts to get to the bus stop had become a major issue, they began to brainstorm what they could do to protect her from leaving the premises but give her the illusion of freedom. They finally came up with a simple but ingenious idea. The staff moved a comfortable bench from the back of the nursing home to the front of the home near the entrance. On the back of the bench, which is the first thing the patient would see when she walked out the door, was a sign that read "bus stop". Rather than constantly fight with their patient, they would utilise what she already was doing to ensure she did not go far and remained safe until someone could assist her.

The plan worked because the staff would look out and see the patient sitting on the bench at the front of the home waiting or the "bus". The staff would then go outside and let the patient know the bus was running late. They would then ask the patient if she wanted to go inside and they would call her when the bus was near the nursing home. The patient, without any hassle, would go back inside and eventually forgot about going home on the bus for a little while.

Instead of fighting our clients we can use what they give us to help create a healing process. If we continue to try to force our clients to assume our worldview, we end up wearing ourselves out and do little more than strain the therapeutic relationship. When we get a client who presents to us a behaviour that appears difficult to directly change, we might need to ask ourselves how we can use what she is giving us in a creative way.

I worked with a family whose six-year-old son had decided he was no longer a little boy. He had decided he was a dog. He acted like a dog all the time. He would constantly walk around on all fours and would bark instead of talk. He would not respond to any commands to stop his dog-like behaviour. This had been going on for over a month and was really distressing his parents. They had, in their words, tried everything to get him to start acting like a boy again. The boy even behaved like this at school, which had resulted in the school calling the parents to take him home as he was disrupting the class with his odd behaviour.

I met the parents alone in our session, as they did not feel they could bring their son due to his behaviour. I found the parents to be very pleasant but extremely passive people who catered far too much to their son's behaviour. For example, in our discussions I learned that if their son did not want to eat a certain meal, they would change the menu to accommodate him. They would also consult the son on what he wanted to do during the day and change their plans around the son so he would be "happy" and enjoy his day. Their son was very catered for and was surprisingly not worse than he could have been since he was in charge of the family.

I did not think that I could directly do anything to get the boy to stop being a dog so I decided to utilise what the boy was already doing to help him become a boy again. I told the parents I could help them but it was crucial they follow my instructions. I let them know they would be very uncomfortable doing the assignment I was going to give them but if they followed through they would be helping their son more than they could ever imagine. I then told them their son was indeed a dog and they as parents needed to accept his decision to be a dog. I directed them to begin allowing this behaviour and treating him like a dog. The first thing I recommended was to remind the parents and the boy that many dogs sleep not in comfortable beds but outside in the dark. I also reminded the family that dogs eat dog food, not human food. I let them know that dogs aren't supposed to have children's toys, watch television, or be able to get on the furniture.

The parents eventually understood where I was coming from and they decided, with some of my playful prodding, to make some changes in the home starting that day. When the parents returned home they informed the boy that since he was a dog he was to only be fed dry dog food and water, which they placed on the floor by the dining room table for him. The boy was none too pleased about his new dietary choice and did not eat any of his "food". That evening the parents instructed the boy that he was to sleep outside on the doormat on the back porch. The boy was let out of the house into the nice spring evening and the light promptly turned off, as one would do with a dog. His parents secretly watched him through a window to ensure he was safe. After an hour went by, the boy became a little fearful of the dark and developed a dislike for the hard porch. He knocked on the door and asked to be let in. At first his parents stated they could not let a dog into the house. With some slight crying and pleading by the child to affirm he was a boy and not a dog, he was let into the house and never became a dog again.

Reframing

Reframing is a form of utilisation in which the problem the client brings to therapy is incorporated into the process of solving the problem. Reframing can be defined as a method in which the therapist restates or reinterprets the client's problem whereby the client can experience the problem in a new way. By directing the client to experience the problem from other points of view, the therapist can change the meaning and definition of the problem into one that will be a little easier to solve. Reframing can take the form of therapeutic conversation or behavioural tasks. If successful, this creates a new frame in which more varied ways of understanding the problem are discovered.

An easy way to understand reframing is to imagine that one of your clients brings a framed picture to therapy. The frame the client has placed around the picture is labelled "problem". You notice this picture would be enhanced by a more attractive frame. You take the client's picture out of the "problem" frame and place it into a different frame labelled "resource". The picture has not changed but the frame that holds the picture is now different, which creates a different perception of the picture on the part of the client. In the client's state of mind she could only envision one type of frame for her picture until you shared with her the other choices available.

In the classic book on brief therapy *Change* (Watzlawick, Weakland, & Fisch, 1974), the authors, who were very influenced by Erickson, state that when a therapist uses reframing he "changes the conceptual order and/or emotional setting or viewpoint in relation to which a situation is experienced" and as a result "changes its entire meaning" (p. 95). In their view reframing is a very useful tactic to aid in persuading clients to change their course of action where previously they would be unwilling or unable to do so.

The point of using reframing in a therapy session is to change a client's view of the problem from something as being unsolvable, into a new experience in which the problem is something that can be changed and maybe even appreciated. Think of reframing as a way to suggest to your client a more resourceful and meaningful experience in which she can have access to different behaviour and emotions. Reframing should give your client new possibilities that she had not previously considered or experienced.

Erickson utilised the frames his clients would present in a way that activated the inner resources the clients already possessed. He believed the clients he worked with "have problems because of learned limitations. They are caught in mental sets, frames of reference and belief systems that do not permit them to explore and utilise their own abilities to the best advantage." (Erickson & Rossi, 1980, p. 38). He believed that "when you can force people to get beyond the immediate confines of an emotional configuration and look at something objectively, they get a different view and then there is nothing they can do about that new understanding they develop" (Haley, 1973, p. 247).

Erickson once worked with a man who had recently been married but became impotent on his wedding night. This was very distressing to the man and his bride. Every time this man would want to consummate his marriage he was inhibited by his impotence. He continued to have this issue for the next couple of weeks. It eventually got to the point in which the woman he married had gone to see an attorney about seeking an annulment. Erickson requested a session with the man's wife to discuss the distressing issue of her husband's impotence.

The woman came to her session with Erickson and was very direct about the issue and she was very angry with her new husband. Erickson listened to her side of the story and then asked her what she felt about the compliment her husband was paying her. The woman was very confused by Erickson's framing of her husband's impotence as a compliment. Erickson then told her it was apparent to him that her husband found his new wife's body so beautiful that he became overwhelmed and as a result could not perform. Erickson then brought the husband into the session and related the same comment to him. The couple left Erickson's office with a new perspective of the husband's impotence. They later informed Erickson that after leaving his office they could hardly wait to get home in order to have sex. After that one session they had no more need of assistance as the husband's problem disappeared (Haley, 1973).

How to reframe

Notice your client's present interpretation of the problem. Ask yourself what other possible interpretation of the problem could exist. For example, if a client is having issues with anger outbursts, a therapist could view this response as a way to teach her family how to access and be comfortable with all their emotions. Is this problem something that would be appropriate in another setting? If the context of the problem changed would it still be a problem for the client? For example, the anger outbursts would be very beneficial to exhibit if the client was being harassed or intimidated in a dangerous situation. Find the most interesting reframe and immediately point it out to the client. The reframe could be something that is humorous, profound, or just plain odd. Notice how the reframe affects the client. If it works build on it, if not then discard it.

The most important thing in designing a reframe to a problem is whether the reframe really resonates with the client or not. I have often observed that the client may sit quietly with a look of contemplation after a reframe of the problem as she processes a new understanding that never occurred to her.

Examples of reframes

> Anger outburst—brave enough to show emotion
> Being oppositional—courage to stick to one's opinion
> Fearful—the ability to recognise danger faster than others
> Impulsive behaviour—not afraid of experiencing spontaneity
> Overly controlling—adept at maintaining structure in one's life
> Easily distracted—the ability to notice multiple perspectives
> Feeling weak—strong enough to show weakness
> Resistance to speaking about a specific topic—desire to have freedom
>   to discuss what one wants.

The very action of reframing the manner in which a client perceives the problem can have a major impact on the outcome of therapy. I once worked with a woman who reluctantly came to therapy due to her hearing the voice of "the devil". Peggy was the wife of a fundamentalist pastor and was very active in his church. She had been hearing the devil speak to her for some time but lately the voice had become more aggressive and frightening. She said the voice would come upon her at any time and in any place. It had become so scary that Peggy had begun screaming back at the voice to alleviate her fear by telling the devil of her intense faith in Jesus Christ and to leave her alone. This would have been fine at home but she began doing this in public and at church meetings. Even her husband had become more uncomfortable, and worried that the messages his wife was receiving were not from beyond but in her own mind.

Peggy did not feel there was anything mentally ill about her as she and her husband believed in the very real existence of the devil and his mission to corrupt and disrupt all that is good in the world. At the urging of her adult daughter, who had been to college and was more accepting of the explanation that her mother may have auditory hallucinations rather than conversations with the lord of the underworld, Peggy went to the family doctor who referred her to a psychiatrist. Peggy refused medication, telling the psychiatrist that medication was for sick people and she was not sick. She let him know that she was fighting the devil and he is as real as can be. The psychiatrist directed the daughter and Peggy's husband to seek talking therapy for Peggy, which could help if Peggy was refusing medication.

When she walked into my office Peggy told me directly that she did not need to be in therapy and was only going to come this one time. She was showing up for her appointment to please her husband and daughter but she did not believe there was anything wrong with her. I have to admit that I felt a little pressured to assist someone who was having auditory hallucinations in one session. I decided I would just try to be as present and accepting of Peggy as I could, because it appeared to me that she felt frustrated that no one believed her. From her perspective it must have been tough to have her own husband, who was a preacher, not be sure if she was truly experiencing what she thought she was experiencing.

While Peggy told the story of why she was in therapy, I realised there was no way I could convince her that what she was experiencing may not be real. I decided to reframe what was happening since this behaviour may never go away if she was not open to medication and further therapy. After listening to her complaints about the intrusiveness of the devil's commentary, I asked her what specifically the devil stated when he spoke to her. Peggy told me the devil would tell her she was no good and that everything she did was a failure. He told her that she was unlovable and she was never going to amount to anything.

After hearing this, I asked her what was so scary and upsetting about those statements. She looked at me in disbelief and replied, "No one wants to be told those things particularly from the prince of evil!" I agreed with her and then asked her why she believed the devil had taken such an interest in her out of all the billions of people on the planet. Peggy declared that it was the good work on the part of God that made the devil so interested in messing with her. I totally agreed with her assessment of the situation and she was more than a little surprised when I told her that I was not so sure it wasn't the devil talking to her. She seemed somewhat pleased that I did not dismiss her beliefs about this situation.

I sat quietly for a minute and then I asked Peggy, "What do you think the devil would say to you if you were not doing such good work for God?" She thought for a minute and said she didn't think he would say anything to her. I then asked her what she would have to be doing for the devil to say nice things to her. Peggy told me that if the devil was giving her compliments it was a clear sign she was doing something awful and screwing up her connection to God. "Oh, so you are saying the reason the devil is talking to you so much is because you are active in spreading the good work of God and if the devil is saying such hateful things to you it is because you are doing God's will?" Peggy thought for a moment and said that was the case. "So in a way it must be very affirming and even flattering that the devil is so angry that he says such hateful things to you?" I asked her. This reframe appeared to cause a shift in Peggy. She told me she had never thought about the voices this way previously. I told her that the devil probably had not wanted her to learn the true reason he was bothering her.

From that point we began to work on a specific plan to help her deal with the devil's comments to her. She was to remind herself she was safe when she heard the voices as she was doing God's work. If the voices became too intense she was to quietly excuse herself from any social interaction she was involved in at that moment and seek a private place to deal with the devil for a few minutes. This place could be another room, in her car, or outside. I directed Peggy to begin carrying a notepad with her wherever she went so that she could write the devil a note to tell him exactly how she felt. I told her by writing the note she would be making her comments more real to him than just "idle words". I told her to write whatever she wanted in the most extreme wording so she could "give the devil his due".

She was then directed to give the devil a final sign of defiance by taking all the notes she had written and placing them inside her Bible for the night. The next day she was free to dispose of the notes in any manner she chose. I ended our session with the direct order for her not to worry about what her husband and daughter would say as she was doing God's work and extreme situations call for extreme measures. Peggy seemed ready to begin her new mission.

As she had promised in our first meeting, I did only get to see Peggy for one session but a follow-up phone call with her husband two weeks later let me know she was better. Her husband stated that Peggy did indeed still hear the devil talking to her often but she was rarely yelling back as she had previously done. She would usually slip away and write in her notepad. He told me Peggy had even started a separate journal specifically for writing down all the good things that were going on in her life. Peggy's husband told me she seemed a little more relaxed and things around the house had calmed down a bit since she found a new way to interact with the devil.

Reframing can also be effective when working with younger clients. Cade and O'Hanlon (1993) reported an effective intervention using reframing with an aggressive child. A single mother brought her nine-year-old son to therapy due to the child's hostile behaviour towards any of her male friends who visited. The boy would swear and act aggressively towards the men while refusing to leave the mother alone with them. The mother had become afraid to ask any man to come over to visit.

After hearing of the problem the woman was faced with, the therapist told the mother that the boy was actually very sensitive and he was aware of his mother's fears of being hurt and abandoned again. The boy's actions were then reframed as protective measures to safeguard the mother. The therapist told her the boy was testing each man to see if he was someone who loved his mother enough to put up with the boy's bad behaviour. The boy was directly praised for his actions and directed to continue his efforts to protect his mother. When the mother returned to her next session she reported a major improvement in the boy's behaviour. Just by hearing a different perspective on his actions, the boy and his mother shifted their attitudes to the situation that had brought them to therapy.

Paradoxical interventions

Paradoxical interventions could best be described as a therapist directing his client to perform the very problem the client is seeking to eradicate. The underlying principle is that clients implement certain emotions and actions for specific reasons. Usually the behaviour is unconsciously created in order to meet a certain perceived need by the client. Examples of this could be the need to be noticed, the need to feel some degree of control in one's life, the need to feel safe, the need to appear strong, etc.

By directing the client to enact the problem behaviour, the therapist is assisting the client in meeting this need but at the same time realising (consciously or unconsciously) how much control she truly has over the behaviour. The act of consciously creating the behaviour can lead the client to realise that if she can create it, then she also has the ability to change it. As previously stated, it is important for the therapist to maintain a non-judgmental attitude towards the client's behaviour as this acceptance of the behaviour by the therapist allows the problem behaviour to become a beneficial resource in the therapeutic process.

Paradoxical interventions may be used when there is a specific problem that the client believes is involuntary. Often clients perceive certain actions as out of their control even though they have an unconscious strategy of how to create the behaviour. Clients may be directed to increase the frequency of the behaviour or to schedule it for a specific time each day. They may even be directed to increase the intensity of the behaviour. If needed, friends and family members of a client could be recruited to help the client create her behaviour within the new paradigm.

It goes without saying (but I am going to say it anyway) that behaviour directly harmful to the client is not to be used in a paradoxical intervention. Ethically we would not ask a person suffering from drug addiction to triple her use of narcotics or ask someone who is the abuser in a relationship to abuse more. These interventions are to be used only when it is safe and in the framework of a positive therapeutic relationship.

Erickson once worked with a sixteen-year-old girl who sucked her thumb to such a point where her parents, friends, and school officials had attempted everything they could think of to get her to stop. Erickson directed the girl not to give in to other people's wishes and to continue sucking her thumb in a manner that would really upset her parents. He had her suck her thumb for one hour after dinner in the presence of her father while he read in the living room and suck her thumb for one hour in the presence of her mother while she worked in the sewing room. Erickson told her she needed to suck her thumb continuously and as hard as she could during these times.

Over the next four weeks the girl attempted to faithfully follow Erickson's directions but soon found she was growing tired of the regimented schedule of thumb sucking and began shortening her thumb-sucking performances for her parents more and more until she eventually stopped. She then became interested in more normal adolescent activities (Haley, 1973).

I believe one of the main reasons paradoxical interventions can be so effective is that it is another method of reframing how the client experiences a problem. The client is expecting the therapist to help change a certain situation but when the therapist actually directs the client to intentionally perform the situation it sets the client up for a different experience. Previously the client may have felt out of control due to the problem but after performing the behaviour in a different manner or setting, the behaviour can then be framed to the client as a controllable action that can be altered.

Once I used a paradoxical intervention when working with a couple who came to therapy due to the husband's drinking. The wife, who seemed very worried and anxious, told me her husband was drinking ten beers a night. The husband verified this but insisted that, in spite of his herculean consumption, he was not an alcoholic because he could control his drinking. He pointed out that he could go all day at work without drinking a drop. He felt "real alcoholics" couldn't stop drinking during the working day. He stated he just liked to drink his beer at night and was tired of his wife complaining and nagging about it.

I asked the husband how many beers a night an alcoholic would drink. He said he thought an alcoholic would probably drink more than twelve beers a night. I agreed with him that alcoholics tend to drink a lot more than most people. I then asked if "real alcoholics" could cut down on their drinking for consistently long periods. The husband stated he felt alcoholics would not be able to cut down on their drinking at all. I told him I totally agreed with him.

At this point I told the husband I did not want him to stop drinking. The wife's eyes were wide and her jaw dropped. The husband looked equally shocked as he expected to have to fight with the therapist about whether or not he was an alcoholic. I told both of them that I felt the husband was very clear on what an alcoholic was and I knew a way he could prove to his wife that he was not an alcoholic without giving up his favourite beverage. The husband looked very happy and intrigued to hear this surprising announcement.

I directed the husband to feel free to drink as soon as he got home but he could only drink four beers a night. I directed the wife to buy a small portable cooler in which the beer was to be placed. She was instructed to pack this cooler with four beers from the refrigerator as soon as her husband came home and give the cooler to him for the evening. The husband was supposed to enjoy the beer in the cooler but not the beer in the refrigerator. I told the couple that since the husband would be cutting his drinking back by more than half for three weeks, this should be proof to the wife that her husband was not an alcoholic as, according to the husband, "real alcoholics" cannot cut down their drinking for a long period.

The wife was told to leave her husband alone and let him drink. I also told her to count the number of beers in the refrigerator when her husband came home and to re-count them first thing in the morning to prove to herself that her husband was only drinking four beers a night. I looked at the husband with a smile and said, "This won't be hard because you're not an alcoholic and you can control how many drinks you have a day. I believe you will have some relief in showing your wife proof that you can control yourself and, if nothing else, you won't be nagged about your enjoyment of drinking." I ended the session with a commitment from both of them to see me again in three weeks to let me know how things were going.

Three weeks later the couple reappeared in my office. The wife who had looked so worried and frustrated earlier appeared to be more centred and calm. The husband, on the other hand, acted slightly timid and ashamed when we started our session. The wife related how they had followed my directives. Within two nights she had caught her husband attempting to sneak into the refrigerator for another beer after he had finished his nightly assigned four beers. He claimed that he miscounted the number of beers she had prepared for him and thought he was a beer short. Two mornings later she counted the beers in the refrigerator to find several missing from the previous night. The couple began have more intense arguments as it became apparent the husband was not honouring the agreement of only four beers a night.

By the second week the husband was attempting to sneak off to buy beer but was caught with a beer can in his truck by his wife. The husband told his wife that he was not interested in playing any more "shrink games" and just wanted to be treated like an adult and left alone. The wife reminded him it was he who stated "real alcoholics" couldn't cut down their drinking for long periods. This culminated in more arguments and the husband sleeping on the couch.

In our next session the wife related that her husband finally had to admit he could not stop drinking at just four beers. At this point the husband spoke up and said he didn't feel he was a "real alcoholic" but he did want to get some help to deal with the amount of beer he wanted to drink. Therapy proceeded with a new focus, which could not have come about so quickly if the husband's symptoms had not been paradoxically utilised. He continued to make improvements in his reduction of alcohol in addition to becoming more open to discussing other aspects of his life that bothered him.

CHAPTER THREE

Altering patterns

E rickson often said that the reason people continue in the same dysfunctional ways of interacting with the world was due to their lack of flexibility. He felt that the more flexible clients could become, the easier it would be for them to change. In order to create a shift in clients' maladaptive behaviour, therapists need to design inter-ventions that give clients more flexible responses to their problems. Just the act of giving clients an extra degree of flexibility could cause some portion of their symptom to change (O'Hanlon, 1987).

An analogy to this approach would be when one makes a cake. If the ingredients of a cake (flour, sugar, eggs, milk, etc.) are altered in any way, the cake will be different. It will still be a cake but not the same cake as the one with the set pattern of ingredients. For example, if I was making a cake and I added three times the amount of milk the recipe called for, the cake would not be as firm as I might like. If I left out sugar when making the cake it would probably not have much taste to it. If I added salt instead of sugar, then probably no one would want to eat it. In all these scenarios we can still call it a cake but it would certainly not be the same as if we followed the original recipe.

Clients have a recipe for how they do or feel things. If we want to get them to change the outcome of their behaviour we need to give them a different recipe. Client behaviour needs to be seen not as pathology but rather as a process. When we give our clients a new process to perform it is not uncommon for the old problem to discontinue operating the same way. If we ask a couple who consistently fight at the dinner table to continue fighting but to do it standing on their dining room chairs, it changes the process of how they fight, which may lead to other surprising changes in their interactions.

Altering the manner in which a client performs her process of a problem is often one of the simplest ways to create change. Sometimes it does not have to be a huge shift in a pattern to have a dramatic effect. Erickson would often direct clients to perform small changes that would snowball into greater shifts in their lives. By altering how his clients performed their processes he was able to change the context in which the problems occurred. Rather than force on a client a massive new action, which they may resist, Erickson believed that adjusting even just one part of the process creates the possibility for change in other areas of the problem. He felt that no matter how small the disruption of a pattern was, it could have far-reaching consequences for how and if the client continued to perform her "problem" in the future.

In a classic example of this concept, Erickson once worked with a man who told Erickson that he could not urinate unless he was able to do so through a tube that was eight to ten inches long. The man was instructed to make a tube from bamboo that was twelve inches long and to use that to urinate through instead. He then suggested to the man that he shorten the tube's length a little at a time over the next few days or weeks. The man shortened the tube over several weeks until he decided to get rid of it entirely (O'Hanlon & Hexum, 1990).

Another example of Erickson's penchant for playing with patterns can be seen through his work with a young boy who had a thumb-sucking issue. This boy would only suck the thumb of his left hand. Erickson let the boy know he was not being fair to the fingers on his other hand and he was to begin sucking his right thumb. This led to the boy breaking his pattern and becoming more open to ceasing his habit (O'Hanlon & Hexum, 1990).

This approach to altering patterns requires the therapist to see the problem the client brings into therapy as a dynamic process the client is actively performing. If some part of the process is changed, the client will not be able to have the problem the same way. It is very important to get as much precise, detailed information from the client as possible, on how she experiences the problem. The therapist needs to know when the problem occurs, where it happens, who is with the client when the problem occurs, the length of time the problem lasts, and any other small details that could make a difference when adjusting the process of the problem.

Cade and O'Hanlon (1993) relate a case in which a woman sought counselling for drinking too much alcohol. This woman was directed to drink as much as she wanted as long as she would take off all her clothes and then put them on back to front before taking a drink. If the woman wanted another drink she was to perform the same action. After only one week the woman reported she had begun to control her drinking and that she found the whole process amusing.

I often ask clients to give me an in-depth, sensory-based movie review of their problem in which they are to tell me exactly what is happening as if they were watching a movie of the problem occurring. I ask them to tell me what is happening in the "movie scene" that is their problem. I get information about the setting, the actors, the dialogue, and the scripts used in the construction of the problem movie. By having clients describe these aspects of the situation, they will often view themselves in their mental movie. This part of the process alone can create a shift in clients as it slightly dissociates them from the problem, as they have become a third-party observer. Sometimes they might even notice small ways they can change the outcome of the problem, which had not occurred to them previously when they were experiencing the problem first hand.

When gathering information to be used in changing a pattern, we have to assume every detail is important. There are three main areas of information that need to be obtained before changing the manner in which the client performs the problem.

When does it happen?

Ask about the specific day and time(s) of the day the problem happens. What time does the problem not happen?

Where does it happen?

Ask about the location(s) the problem occurs. Where is the person when the problem happens? Where does the problem not happen?

With whom does it happen?

Ask about other parties involved in the performance of the problem. Who is around when the problem happens? Who is not around when the problem happens?

Often the client will state they do not know the in-depth answers to these questions as they feel their actions are automatic. Usually upon kindly pressing clients to think about the questions they will come up with answers. If they immediately without thought say, "I don't know," I usually reply by validating them but still asking for the answer by saying, "I know you don't know but if you did know what would you see?" Most of the time clients are then able to focus a little more easily on finding the answers.

The following six methods are a streamlined application for using Erickson's concepts of pattern alteration. Erickson used many more than these six patterns but these are the ones I have found most effective and easiest to implement. For a more thorough listing of the use of pattern alteration, consult O'Hanlon (1999). I have found these to be the most common methods but by all means don't be bound to only these six. Experiment and see what works for you.

Six methods to alter patterns

Changing when the pattern happens

Often a client will perform a less than desirable behaviour pattern at a consistent time or in a similar situation. The client may become angry when a specific situation occurs or at a particular time of the day. If the therapist can alter when the pattern occurs then the client will have to perform the behaviour in a different way, which gives her some flexibility in behaviour. As stated previously, when the client is given more flexibility it is much easier for her to create change in her life.

I once worked with a couple who constantly argued about how the finances were handled. The husband was very knowledgeable about money and usually did a good job in handling the couple's investments. The wife felt shut out of the decision-making process as her husband was much more capable with their finances. The wife also got exasperated when he attempted to show her what was going on with their finances, as she believed it was beyond her comprehension. The most consistent thing about their arguments was that they took place in the evenings. This is the only time they discussed money-related issues.

I instructed this couple to only discuss money issues between 5:30 am and 6:30 am. The couple's usual time to get up in the morning was 6:30 am. Not only was getting up an hour earlier a hassle, it also changed the way they discussed money. Even though there were a few heated exchanges initially, they were both able to begin regulating their emotions about money discussions. It may have been the freshness of the new day or that both of them were too tired to argue but either way changing when the discussions took place altered their pattern of knee-jerk reactions when going over their financial statements.

Changing where the pattern happens

Sometimes changing the location of where a problem occurs can create a break in the pattern. There can be locations that can act as triggers for certain behaviour and when those triggers are not available the pattern will either have to change or it will stop. By moving the behaviour to a different location we do two things: first we remove the client(s) from the trigger; and second we create a short break in the pattern. People are often more comfortable walking on a path that is well worn. Even if the path is fraught with danger, many people are comfortable only walking on this one path. It can feel odd or dangerous when they think about embarking on a new path. However, once people walk on a new path few times, they quickly get used to it and realise they now have another way of getting to where they want to go.

For example, I once worked with a couple who fought almost every evening after dinner. They were nice people who just could not seem to stop themselves from engaging in the incredible intensity of their loud arguments. After talking with them for a while I learned that both of them really worried that the neighbours would hear their arguments and think badly of them. It was very important to each of them to have a good reputation in their community. They had both worked really hard to be seen as an ideal couple. They wanted to project an image of being stable people who were successful in all areas of their lives.

When I learned this, I directed them to agree to cease arguing inside the home after dinner. They could continue arguing but only if they argued outside their home in full view of their neighbours. They reluctantly agreed to change the location of their arguments. At their next session two weeks later they disclosed that they had argued less and at a much-subdued volume. Even when they did not follow the directive to go outside to have an argument, they noticed the intensity of the arguments had considerably decreased. Fairly quickly they began to alter how they communicated their feelings to each other to a more positive and effective way.

At a training seminar I remember a therapist describing his experience of working with a couple who were constantly fighting and appeared to be unable to cease their daily onslaught of anger and resentment. The therapist's intervention was not to ask the couple to stop fighting but rather for them to go to the bathroom when a fight started. The husband was directed to take off all his clothes and lie in the bath. The wife was directed to sit on the toilet. Only then could they continue their argument. As expected, within a short time the change in the pattern of their altercations led to the diminishing of the arguments. Their children even picked up on what was happening and would sometimes point to the bathroom when any verbal interaction between the couple began to sound heated.

Erickson once worked with a young man named Tom who reported feeling loneliness, boredom, and depression. He would sit alone inside all day doing nothing. Erickson directed him to feel free to be as lonely as possible but he had to do it at the local library. Erickson told Tom if he was going to feel alone and bored he might as well do it elsewhere. Tom followed Erickson's directive and went to the library. Out of boredom, he began looking at magazines about caving. Within a short time, someone at the library noticed he was reading about caving and began talking to him about going on a caving trip. Tom eventually went on the trip and began to make new friends and take on new hobbies (O'Hanlon & Hexum, 1990).

Changing the duration of the pattern

When a client presents a problem to the therapist, the therapist might want to ask how long it takes the client to perform the specific behaviour she wishes to change. For some clients the problem they bring to therapy only lasts a few minutes. Others may present a problem that lasts several hours. When we know the length of time the client performs the problem we can begin to immediately shift the pattern by asking the client to shorten or lengthen the action. By altering even just a little part of the pattern the client will know the problem is not something that is set in stone and it can be changed.

Erickson used this strategy when he worked with a teenage boy with learning difficulties. The boy had a compulsion to wave his right arm in front of him 135 times per minute. Erickson directed the boy to begin increasing the rate to 145 waves per minute and then to return to 135 waves per minute. Through several sessions Erickson had the boy increase the rate of his waving by five extra waves and then had him decrease his waving by ten waves. This continued until the boy ceased waving at all. Gradually shifting the boy's pattern gave him the opportunity to realise that the pattern could be altered and eliminated (Erickson & Rossi, 1980).

I once worked with a man who had developed an obsessive pattern of having to touch a door knob seven times every time he used it. Even though it was not a major compulsion he still felt trapped by having to touch the knob so many times. He told me that he had a horrible feeling that something terrible would happen if he didn't do it. The times he did force himself not to touch the door knob seven times he began to have a panic attack that was only stopped when he touched the knob the required number of times. No matter what door he used he felt like he had no choice but to perform his ritual.

I told him that I was not going to tell him to stop touching the door so many times. I was, however, going to direct him to begin touching the door thirty times instead of seven. The man was very surprised and perplexed by this directive. He reluctantly went along with it. He did not want to have to touch the door knob that many times but he was willing to try it. Every time he opened a door he had to touch the door knob thirty times no matter how long it took.

When I saw him two weeks later he told me that he really had tried to touch the door knob thirty times each time he used a door but he grew tired of performing of the action. He was surprised to find out that by the end of the first week he only needed to touch the door five times instead of seven. By the time he came into the next session he was only touching the door knobs twice. By altering the duration of his pattern this man was able to become flexible enough to begin limiting the amount of time he invested in his problem. He decided he could live with having to touch the door knob twice and felt therapy had been a success.

Adding to the pattern

Sometimes therapists work with clients who appear unable, for one reason or another, to cease or disrupt any aspect of their problem. In this case, the therapist can utilise what the clients are already doing and add another component to the action. The therapist will direct the clients to continue the performance of the problem but will give them another action to do along with the problem in order to create a change in the problem's performance. In this manner of working the therapist does not have to directly engage in a power struggle with the clients over the desire to eliminate the problem behaviour. Instead the therapist may appear to agree with the clients about the problem being too difficult to stop immediately. The insistence of the therapist for the clients to continue their present problematic behaviour may in itself be a pattern interruption in what clients expect to hear from their therapist. Clients may be more open to adding another component to the pattern if they feel the therapist is not directly forcing them to cease their problem behaviour.

Erickson once worked with a retired police officer who had become very obese in addition to smoking and drinking. Erickson directed the man to purchase cigarettes only one pack at a time and in order to obtain them he had to walk a substantial distance to buy them at a specific store. Erickson also directed the man to only buy his groceries from a store that was half a mile away. The man was only to buy what he needed for each meal. Lastly, Erickson allowed the man to continue his drinking as long as he walked one mile per drink. This adjustment to the way in which the man performed his eating, drinking, and smoking was sufficient to create space for him to change his behaviour. By walking every day he lost weight and decreased the frequency of his drinking and smoking (Rosen, 1991).

I was able to use this pattern alteration technique with a mother and daughter who sought therapy to cease their intense, hour-long arguments and shouting. When the mother, daughter, and father first came to see me it was obvious that intense emotions existed between mother and daughter. It was also apparent how truly exhausted the father was due to the constant fighting at home. He looked as if he hadn't slept in days.

The family said that every evening the mother and daughter would find something about which to argue intensely. According to the father, these arguments would go on for an hour or two and would culminate with horrible name calling and screaming. After the argument both parties would storm off and cease speaking to each other for the rest of the night (but would each seek out the poor father to complain about the other's behaviour). The topics of the arguments could be anything: what was for dinner, the daughter's boyfriend, the mother's clothes, what would be watched on television that evening, etc. The father said that he had grown so tired of the arguing that he intentionally began working later at the office in the hope of avoiding some of the evening drama.

Both the mother and daughter said they wished to cease arguing and both of them immediately defended their actions. Both said that there was no reason to argue but that the other created the whole situation and there was no way either of them could control their verbal interactions. The more I asked each party to explain to me how specifically she could adjust her behaviour, the more each one blamed the other. This ended up with a really loud argument in my office, which enabled me to have a front row seat to the family dynamics in real time. As the mother and daughter argued in my office I looked over at the father and noticed he looked even more tired.

As the argument continued for a little while, I picked up on both the mother and daughter repeatedly saying things during their spat like, "You just can't let me *win*", "I can't *win* with you can I?" and "I am not going to *lose* any more of my time on this." After I was able to get the mother and daughter to quieten down a little, I told them that I had a task for them to do for me but I only wanted them to agree to do it if they really, truly wanted to "win" at ceasing their arguments. I made sure I told them that I would not be asking them to stop their arguments.

They seemed intrigued and agreed to do as I directed. I instructed both of them to feel free to continue arguing but they could only argue if both of them held their arms straight up towards the ceiling, like a referee does in American football when a team scores a touchdown. They could argue as long or as intensely as they wanted, so long as their arms were held straight up. If either one of them began to drop their arms even a little bit, the argument had to stop on both sides until both parties could return to fully holding their arms straight up. I recruited the father to watch the arguments closely and to let both of them know if one of their arms began to lower. I half-jokingly told them that they could make it a game to see who could argue the most intensely while holding their arms up as it would be interesting to see who was able to "win" this event.

After two weeks the family returned to therapy to report that although the arguments were still occurring they were less frequent and less intense. By having to hold their arms in the air the arguments became more of a chore and the two women tried to find ways to not have a full-blown argument. In addition, holding their arms up high caused fatigue fairly quickly and the arguments had to have short breaks while one or both rested their arms. These short breaks allowed a pause in the non-stop barrage of animosity for which the family had sought help. Holding their arms over their head also distorts the diaphragm, affecting the volume of the exchange. The mother even said that as soon as she and her daughter began to start raising their voices, the father would appear out of nowhere to sit in the room and stare at both of them to see whose arms would begin to lower first. The daughter even admitted to finding out she was able to let many more things her mother said or did go by without comment due to her realising how little good came from the arguing. I told them how proud I was of them following through on their assignment and I felt that this was a family that was going to "win the game of therapy".

Breaking up the pattern

Instead of addressing the client's problem in its totality, the therapist might only need to address one aspect of the problem at a time. This can make the problem more manageable and less overwhelming for the client. The therapist can often shift the performance of the pattern by working on one very small part of it. By breaking up the flow of the pattern the outcome can change in surprising ways.

A couple once sought therapy from me for help in ending their loud, aggressive arguing. They seemed pleasant people who were motivated to seek help with their issue. Once the session began this couple unleashed an extremely loud and vicious round of arguing that surprised me. The intensity of the argument began rising very quickly. I usually let a couple argue for a little while in order to allow me to spot patterns and dynamics in their interactions but the speed with which the argument was escalating and the volume of the exchange motivated me to stop the argument. I had heard many couples fight in my office but these two were unlike any couple I had worked with before.

The problem was this couple was so entangled in the argument they could not hear my pleas for them to stop. I found myself escalating my volume very rapidly as well but it was to no avail as they kept going with their fighting. As images of uncomfortable looks exchanged by clients and staff in the waiting room danced in my mind, I knew there was very little hope for this couple to be able to break their pattern without some out of the ordinary action taking place. Unless there was something taking place to stop them in their tracks these people would continue fighting until the very end.

After I had done almost everything that usually works to end arguments, I decided on something a little more drastic. With both hands I grabbed my throat and began choking intensely. I began shaking my body as if I were choking to death. As soon as the couple noticed what I was doing they immediately stopped their heated exchange. When they stopped, I stopped choking. They asked me if I was all right and I told them I was. I then immediately went right into asking them questions about their argument with no mention of my choking. This seemed to disorient them a little but it also temporarily broke their pattern.

After a few minutes the couple seemed to regain their pattern and again launched into a heated exchange. Like clockwork I began choking again which caused the couple to stop and check on me again. After reassuring them I was fine I immediately went back into discussing their relationship. A couple of minutes later they resumed arguing, and again I began choking. By now they had figured out what I was doing so they continued to argue while I choked. I decided that I was not going to be outdone by my clients so I choked so violently that I fell out of the chair, at which point they stopped their argument and demanded to know why I continued to perform this odd, scary action.

I said I felt choked out in the session by the extreme loudness they were exhibiting. From that point on whenever the session began to get a little heated all I had to do was act like I was reaching for my throat and they both ceased the intensity of their exchanges. It was a variation of Pavlov's dog. Towards the end of the session, after the interactions between them had changed for the better, the husband made a pointed statement to the wife using a sharp tone reminiscent of the manner he'd used in their previous heated exchanges. The wife grabbed her throat and all three of us laughed.

By breaking up the pattern of their arguments, even just in one session, the couple was able to experience what it would be like to have their problem in a different way. In the following weeks the couple reported less arguing and more civil discussions between them. There were still some heated arguments between them but they now found it a little easier to control the intensity and duration of their exchanges.

In an inventive example of breaking up a pattern, Erickson worked with a man who had a fear of travelling past the city limits of his home. If he did go past the city limits he would become ill and lose consciousness. Erickson had the man drive to the edge of the city at a very early hour. He was then to stop his car when he reached the city limits. The man was directed to lie down in a ditch near the road until his nausea ceased. Then he was directed to drive only to the next telephone pole and repeat his action of lying in the ditch. Erickson told the man to continue this pattern at every telephone pole he came to on his drive.

The man did the task but eventually got tired of how long it took, of having to lie in the ditch while wearing his good clothes, and of the overall ridiculous nature of the directive, that he decided to just continue driving without stopping. As a result he was able to drive where he wanted without losing consciousness from that point on (Haley, 1973).

Reversing the pattern

Instead of fighting the pattern clients give the therapist, it may be easier to ask them to perform their usual pattern but in a backwards fashion. By reversing the way they perform their behaviour, not only does it give clients more flexibility in how they perform the behaviour but it will also aid in making them fully aware of all the steps required in performing the action.

For example, Evelyn would get into frequent arguments with her family where she would go into a short rage that culminated with her throwing things against the wall. This pattern had progressed to the point where the family would hide any valuable possessions in case Evelyn would lose her temper, throw one of the possessions, and break it. Their house was filled with holes in the walls due to her explosive outbursts. Evelyn did indeed feel out of control and as if she was unable to manage her actions. She said she would go into a rage, lose all focus, and detach from what was going on around her. She only realised she had thrown something right after it hit the wall. Upon seeing the damage she had caused, Evelyn would then immediately calm down and feel really bad about what she had done.

Evelyn and her family were directed to have something available for Evelyn to throw that would not damage the walls. For the next two weeks the family was instructed to give Evelyn that specific something to throw at the wall as soon as it appeared she was getting angry. After she threw the object at the wall she was directed to continue being angry as long as she felt she needed.

The family found some soft foam balls for Evelyn to use that would not damage anything or anyone if thrown at full force. Over the next two weeks the family gave her a foam ball at the first sign of her exasperation turning into full anger. She began throwing the foam balls and then talking about what had made her so angry. Over a short period of time she began to feel less inclined not only to throw things when she became angry but also less inclined to become angry in the first place. By reversing Evelyn's pattern of becoming angry, going into a rage, and then throwing something, she was able to see that she had more options than an automatic response of making holes in the walls of her family's home.

* * *

These methods of pattern alterations can be implemented fairly easily as long as we make sure we thoroughly understand the process our clients use to maintain their problems. In order to have successful outcomes with these unique interventions, it is important for therapists to have an excellent rapport with any client they ask to do something that may be seen as odd. If clients know the therapist has their best interests at heart they are usually open to exploring other ways of responding to the issues they bring with them to therapy. Altering patterns can be effective with a variety of problems. I have found it remarkable how easily some people are able to change what they perceive as an unalterable problem just by shifting one part of it.

CHAPTER FOUR

Multilevel communication

In the past several years many in the psychotherapy field have been influenced by a model of therapy that mostly emphasises the conscious world of the client. From this perspective, the most important area a therapist needs to consider in treating clients is the conscious mind and the analysing, judging, and thinking it performs. This model of therapy is usually done with excluding or ignoring the potential ally in healing that resides in the client's unconscious mind.

Practitioners from the Ericksonian perspective strongly believe that the involvement of the unconscious mind is extremely important for generative change to occur in therapy. An Ericksonian therapist acknowledges that the unconscious is involved in the process of therapeutic change. Erickson believed that through the therapy process the therapist can offer the unconscious the freedom to experience unique, flexible ways of resolving problematic issues (Havens, 1996).

The role of the unconscious in psychotherapy was not a new idea when Erickson began his work. At this time psychotherapy was predominately psychodynamic in nature. Followers of Freud viewed the unconscious mind as a repository for thoughts, desires, and ideas that were socially unacceptable. He also believed the unconscious mind was a psychic storehouse for disturbing emotions and that memories of a traumatic nature were repressed.

Unlike other theorists of his time, Erickson viewed the unconscious not as a mental reservoir that contained a variety of disturbing, socially unacceptable desires that were kept out of awareness due to their threatening nature. Instead, he saw the unconscious as a vast source of innate wisdom that can be accessed by clients to aid them in achieving their goals. He believed the unconscious holds memories in which a considerable supply of positive resources are available to be utilised and to aid in healing.

In using the client's unconscious in therapy, Erickson was aware that the unconscious processes information differently to the conscious mind. He often found that the unconscious could process information symbolically instead of only literally (Zeig & Munion, 1999). Erickson did not believe the therapist's role was to provide clients with insight and interpretation as he felt these did not lead to generative changes in emotions and behaviour. Instead he believed that the therapist's role was to assist clients in using their unconscious minds to have new experiences and that these experiences would lead to changes. Erickson believed there were always two clients in the session: the client's conscious awareness and unconscious awareness (Argast, Landis, & Carrell, 2001).

Erickson found that talking to both the conscious and unconscious in a form of multilevel communication made it more likely that the client would accept the information being presented, than would methods that only used conscious instruction. As Dolan (1985) has pointed out, often when clients receive a therapeutic directive that is recognised on the unconscious level, the client is then free to unconsciously respond in ways that can affect behaviour and emotions. The client does not have to adjust anything on the conscious level, which avoids endless confrontations and challenges that may break rapport, lead to resistance, and hamper the flow of interaction between client and therapist.

Therapeutic stories

Erickson's use of metaphors, stories, riddles, and analogies is often considered one of his most considerable offerings to the world of counselling (Zeig, 1980). Erickson used these methods of multilevel communication as an indirect way to allow clients to create their own meanings and as a result to solve their own problems (O'Hanlon, 1987). One of Erickson's core beliefs was that people already possessed the knowledge and ability to solve the issues they bring to therapy but that knowledge and ability were being used in a context other than the presenting issue. Erickson felt his job was to move the knowledge and ability the client already possessed from the present context to the problem context (O'Hanlon, 1987).

By using a story that was similar to a situation that the client was going through at the moment, the client could unconsciously access her own natural ability to emotionally heal. When a story or metaphor is associated with deep-rooted emotional and behavioural patterns within the client, it can initiate certain positive internal responses such as curiosity, inner strength, or playfulness, which can become accessible to the client to use in solving her own problem. A good story can be a powerful tool in assisting clients in having new experiences at the unconscious level. If told in a compelling manner, along with a strong sense of rapport between therapist and client, a story can have extraordinary effects on the outcome of therapy.

Erickson was able to seamlessly entwine deep messages designed to assist his clients into his stories. His clients were able to gain helpful unconscious information, which their conscious minds would not resist, as the information was presented in the form of stories that appeared to have little to do with the clients in the therapy room. Erickson believed his clients' unconscious minds would latch on to the hidden meanings and subtle metaphors of the stories and use this information in a way to help clients when the time was appropriate.

Therapeutic stories can be a powerful tool in therapy and can be drawn from almost anywhere. They can come from the therapist's own experiences, from the experiences of other clients, friends, or popular media (newspapers, television, films, etc.), and from great mythic stories of the past. All of us know a good story or two to which our clients can relate. I wholeheartedly encourage any therapist to begin paying attention to the various stories one hears on a daily basis, and to notice which ones jump out as possible therapy tools. According to Gordon (1978), the purpose of therapeutic stories and metaphors is "to provide the client an opportunity to get out of the trees and take a look at the forest he has been wandering around in" (p. 157).

During my time as a college professor, I have learned to collect stories and use them to assist my students in understanding the material we are covering. Once, I was teaching an introductory psychology course to a group of students who were primarily studying trade careers such as welding, electrical engineering, and machinery repair. I was attempting to get them to understand Freud's ideas about how a person can become fixated at a psychological stage of development. I thoroughly described how Freud believed early experiences in life could unconsciously affect a person's present and future behaviour and only when a person uncovers these dark unconscious processes will she be able to adjust her emotions and behaviour. I repeated the main points of the lecture several times to vacant stares from my students. I knew this group was not able to relate to what I was teaching.

Since most of the people in the group were not able to understand what I was talking about I decided to tell them a story about a man I had heard of who was having production issues at a factory where he worked. This man found that the main problem with production was the conveyor belt. It seemed the conveyor belt would stop moving at a specific place most days and this would hold up the entire production line. It wasn't until the man went down deep into the production line that he was able to find where the conveyor belt was getting stuck. He noticed the belt was stuck due to it relying on old, worn-out rollers that were put in years ago. Until those rollers were examined and repaired the belt would continue to stay stuck in that same place. With no further explanation all of the students suddenly understood what fixation was and how it worked in Freud's theory.

Since psychotherapy is known as the talking cure, what better place to tell stories? If a client is struggling to have self-discipline with her finances, the therapist might tell a story about a farmer he knows who always went out of his way to put a small amount of food he collected into storage for the winter as it gave him peace of mind to know the food would be there during the cold season when few plants were growing. I have told the story of the boy who cried wolf to a client who was constantly feigning ending the relationship with her partner but always recanted at the last minute as he was preparing to move out. My hope was to indirectly remind her that her actions have consequences and that one day he may call her bluff and go for good.

It is fairly easy to develop a therapeutic story for a client. In order for the story to be effective it must indirectly address the problem or situation for which the client is seeking help. The therapist will have to listen intensely for certain consistent themes that come up during the therapy session. Once a theme has been recognised by the therapist, he will need to set it in a story in which the main character can perceive the metaphorical problem in a different light. In turn, if the client unconsciously identifies with the main character, she will have a new experience of her problem and may even gain alternative ideas about other choices or responses previously not examined. As we have seen in the chapter on pattern alterations, even a small change in perspective can make a major shift in clients' perceptions of their problem.

The essential aspect of any therapeutic story is that the elements of the story must parallel the characters or situations present in the client's present problem (Gordon, 1978). The easiest method I have found to construct a good therapeutic story is to use the basic information I have gathered from the client and assign the qualities and characters to this information:

Step 1: Learn the problem the client has brought with them to therapy
Step 2: Determine what resources the client needs in order to solve the problem
Step 3: Assign characters in the story similar aspects and situations as the client's problem
Step 4: Allow the main character in the story to obtain the resource or directive needed to change
Step 5: Create an ending in which the character uses those resources to gain a positive outcome.

Even traditional, well-known folk and fairy tales can be effective therapeutic stories. Once I worked with a man who kept making impulsive decisions that often placed him in precarious situations. His intentions were always good but he just didn't take the time to think through his actions before he jumped into a decision. These impulsive decisions had cost him time, money, and friendships. Intellectually he knew he needed to slow down his actions and spend more time in the decision-making process but part of him definitely wanted to move as fast as possible.

In the middle of one of our sessions I told him that he could learn a lot from the popular children's story character Goldilocks. I told him the story of Goldilocks (which he had heard many times previously as a child) with special emphasis on how Goldilocks took her time in discerning which porridge was the best for her before she devoured a whole bowl. She took the time to find out which one was too hot, too cold, or just right. She also took the time to find out which bed was too soft, too hard, or just right before she went to sleep. The client understood the obvious meaning much better than when I had stated directly that he might want to take his time in making important decisions.

Erickson had the special gift of being able to seamlessly and spontaneously interject therapeutic stories into a conversation. For many therapists wanting to learn how to create healing stories, having a template to begin learning this skill is helpful. I have found using the template of Joseph Campbell's "hero's journey" to be very helpful in creating therapeutic tales. According to Campbell (1949), the hero's journey is a narrative pattern that consistently appears in ancient and modern myths and rituals. Campbell believed these mythic narratives were really just variations of a single great story. He also believed the true purpose of the hero's journey was really a way for humans to understand our search for the force that is the source of all things and into which everything will eventually return. I think the process of therapy can also be seen as part of the hero's journey and may even represent the entire journey itself.

Here is a quick overview of Campbell's stages of the hero's journey:

The ordinary world: The hero becomes restless and uneasy. In therapy this stage could be the client becoming aware of a problem in his life.
The call to adventure: Some situation occurs that shakes the foundations of the hero's beliefs or way of life. He is dealing with a major change in his life. This stage can be seen as the client becoming aware of the need to seek help with the problem.
Refusal of the call: The hero becomes frightened of the coming change and avoids exploration into this unknown realm. In therapy our clients are often afraid to embrace needed change and may become resistant to doing things differently.
Meeting with a helper or mentor: The hero comes into contact with someone who holds knowledge and experience that can help him move into the unknown realm that he fears. The helper/mentor aids the hero by supplying training or advice that aids the hero in developing skills and wisdom to deal with the oncoming challenges. This is the role of the therapist.

Crossing the threshold: The hero has been armed with the wisdom from his helper/mentor and leaves his ordinary existence and moves forward into unfamiliar territory. The client embarks on the process of change with directives, teachings and/or support from the therapist.

Trials and tests: The hero is severely tested in the new territory and sometimes stumbles with his new skills and wisdom. During this time the hero may gain allies or additional helpers to assist him in moving through the unknown territory. The client is being exposed to new ways of viewing old situations and different experiences to those previously encountered.

Approach: The hero and allies begin their move towards the major challenge the hero will face. The client and therapist continue to build on the foundation of the work.

The ordeal: The hero confronts his worst fears. The hero's old perceptions and identity shift. The client now has a major change in how he views the original problem.

Reward: The hero obtains the source of what he has been seeking. While this is a joyous period there is also the possibility of losing the source in the future. The client begins to accept his new interactions with the world.

The road back: The hero is working towards completing the journey but may have issues with committing to the last part of the journey. The client may have to deal with unforeseen additional problems.

Resurrection: This is the hero's major confrontation with the death of the old self. If the hero does not succeed, other people close to him will suffer. In the end the hero succeeds and emerges from the confrontation reborn. The client turns a corner in therapy and begins to embrace a new perspective on being in the world.

Return: The hero returns home bringing the source of the treasure sought. The hero is transformed and can aid others with his new-found knowledge. The client internalises all the new experiences he has had in creating a new way of life for himself, and from which others in his life will also benefit.

These stages can relate to the latest adventure film or to our clients' work in therapy. We may even be undertaking this journey as therapists as we move through our professional lives attempting to create our own identity as healers. If we think about our work as therapists, we are clearly embodying the role of mentor/helper in our client's hero journey. This alone can make a therapist think a little differently about the therapy process. The therapist may be the client's wise old wizard who is a necessary element on their "quest". The trials and tribulations (and setbacks) clients have do not make them resistant or difficult clients; rather, it is part of their journey as they are tested and face the challenges leading up to their "ordeal".

From this perspective, the client's depression is no longer just a neurotransmitter issue but rather a voyage into the unknown in which the client will have to face a variety of intense situations that are necessary in order to emerge with an enlightened mind and rejuvenated spirit. A client's emotional battle with past trauma now takes the form of the hero's ordeal; the road back can lead to resurrection as a new person who accepts, forgives, and uses the lessons of the past to forge a new beginning in the world. The challenges faced by the client can be seen as part of an epic myth rather than a disease to be cured or medicated away.

Constructing the story

I had the opportunity to construct a mythical tale using the hero's journey motif when I worked with a client named Lori for a few sessions to deal with her anxiety issues. Lori told me in our first session that she had been sexually molested by her grandfather when she was eleven years old. This incident continued to plague her: now aged twenty-eight, she was having frequent bouts of fear and nervous energy. She was very hesitant about having new experiences and curtailed her daily activities to only things where she was sure of the outcome. Consciously she understood why she was so anxious and also understood the various methods to help her cope with her anxiety.

Lori was motivated to change but she was very resistant to accessing her emotions. Allowing herself to fully feel her emotions was frightening to her. This was due to her distancing herself from her feelings for many years in order to avoid emotions tied to the molestation she endured. I knew she needed to access her hidden buried feelings of safety and security but her conscious mind was too busy running through anxiety-provoking scenarios to allow herself to relax for even a minute. Whenever she began to feel fear-based emotions she would quickly distract herself in less than resourceful ways. I believed it was important for Lori to learn to become comfortable with fear instead of running way. Only by allowing herself to feel afraid would she also gain the resource of feeling brave and strong.

In one of our sessions Lori told me she was having some issues getting her five-year-old daughter to go to sleep sometimes because the child was full of energy in the evening. I saw this as a grand opportunity for me to use multilevel communication to speak both to Lori's conscious and unconscious minds. I told Lori there was a story I had learned to tell small children at bedtime that would enable them to relax more quickly and go to sleep more easily. I told her not only was it a good story to get children to relax but it was a lovely fairy tale. I asked if she would like me to tell her the story so that she could tell it to her energetic daughter at bedtime. She told me she would like any help offered. This is the story I shared with her (I have listed which part of the hero's journey is being applied at the various stages of the story):

There once was a young girl named Ariel. She lived many, many years ago in a faraway kingdom. She lived alone and had to learn to survive on her own. This was because an evil old wizard had taken away her family. This wizard had taken away everything that the girl loved and she felt that she had little left to live for. Ariel had her hands full finding water and food while also doing the cleaning and tidying of her small home. At times Ariel felt overwhelmed, as she was so young when this terrible event happened. She was often very afraid that the evil old wizard would come back to harm her. She would only go outside her small home at certain times of the day carefully watching the skies for any sign of the evil wizard. She began to understand that the wizard had put a curse on her, which would haunt her.

Ordinary world

As Ariel grew she learned more and more about the world around her. She learned to take care of herself and make sure all her needs were met. She found an old well that had clean water for her to drink. She found a place to plant vegetables for her to eat. She had a warm place to sleep in her small home. The forest she lived in had many beautiful flowers and trees. Many animals visited Ariel at her home. The animals would play games with her and bring her gifts from the forest. All seemed to be going nicely for Ariel but she still lived in fear of attack by the evil old wizard.

She spent most of her days looking over her shoulder and thinking about the possibility of the evil wizard returning. This made having fun so difficult for Ariel. She desperately wanted to run into the forest with her animal friends and play in unknown and exciting places but she was too afraid to go past the edge of the forest in case something bad happened. Sometimes she would dream of venturing into the unknown areas of the forest and seeing the vibrant colours and the exotic animals. She could see herself in her dreams enjoying new experiences and sensations only to wake up feeling disappointed that she didn't find the courage to travel to unknown places.

Call to adventure

One day she looked out the window of her home to see someone outside. She jumped back in fear that it could be the evil old wizard returning to attack her. After she took time to calm down she looked out the window again to observe who was really outside. It was an older woman wearing a long white gown. This older woman had a shining glow about her which made her figure stand out from everything around her. The older woman saw Ariel peeking out of the window and called to her, "Ariel, come outside for I have something of great importance to share with you!" Ariel hid behind the curtains when she heard the woman call to her.

Refusal of the call

The woman called out again, "Ariel, come out of your home so that I may give you a magical gift that will protect you." Ariel was still hesitant to go outside so she called back to the old woman, "Who are you and how do you know me?" The old woman laughed and said back to her, "Ariel, I have known you your whole life but I have never had the opportunity to truly meet you until now. Please come out and allow me to give you a gift that will help you in so many ways." Part of Ariel was terrified that this woman was sent to harm her or maybe it was the evil wizard in disguise but another part of her knew the woman was here to help her.

Meeting the mentor

Ariel slowly found the courage to open the door and go outside. The older woman was so kind and beautiful that she radiated a glowing light that fascinated Ariel. The woman said, "Thank you for coming out to see me. I have a magical gift that I would like to give you. It is a special way to protect yourself from the evil old wizard who took away so much from you years ago. This gift will remove the curse he left on you."

Ariel asked her, "How did you know about the wizard?" The older woman just smiled and said, "I was there the day he attacked you and your family but at that time I was powerless to help. It has been my mission to find a way for you to free yourself from the legacy of this evil wizard. The gift I give to you can only be obtained if you cross through the forest tomorrow until you come to a waterfall. Behind the waterfall you will find a magical gift which will keep you from having to fear the evil wizard ever again."

Ariel was excited at the possibility of the gift but terrified of going into the unknown areas of the forest. She began to cry because she felt very torn as to what she wanted to do. Part of her wanted to stay in her safe small home with her animal friends nearby but the other part of her wanted to be set free from the curse of the evil wizard. The older woman wiped Ariel's tears away and told her that she believed in her and that with the older woman's magic Ariel could travel through the dense unknown forest safely.

Ariel agreed to face her fear and begin her journey of travelling through the unknown areas of the forest. The older woman smiled and told Ariel she believed in her. The woman then said to Ariel, in a hushed tone, "The secret to being successful in your journey is to accept your fear while you are in the forest. When you accept your fear you will have great magic." And with that the older woman vanished in a flash of light. Ariel was shocked to see her disappear but the woman's magical exit reinforced Ariel's inner feeling that she had to go through the forest.

Crossing the threshold

Ariel slowly began her trek into the forest. The sky seemed to grow darker every few feet into the forest she went. She heard many strange noises as she moved as quietly as possibly. She constantly looked over her shoulder to make sure she was not being followed.

Trials and tests

It was so dark that Ariel couldn't see where she was stepping. All of a sudden Ariel lost her footing and fell into a deep, dark hole in the ground. She struggled her best to get out of the hole but to no avail. The sky was getting darker and she felt helpless and alone. She became so afraid that she began to cry. All of a sudden she noticed a long dark root hidden in the dirt and mud inside the hole. She wondered if she could use this root to pull herself out of the hole she was in. With great effort and discomfort she pulled herself to the top of the hole and grabbed the edge of a large log to support herself. Once she was out of the hole she realised she was unsure of the direction she was supposed to take to reach the waterfall.

Approach

Ariel was becoming more and more afraid she would be lost forever. As she became aware of her feelings the older woman's words came back to her: "The secret to being successful in your journey is to accept your fear while you are in the forest. When you accept your fear you will have great magic." At first, Ariel hesitated to follow the older woman's advice but she gathered her courage and began to allow herself to feel the fear. As she did this she noticed that it began to disappear. This surprised her and made her wonder what kind of magic this was. She continued moving into the forest. She began to smell water and followed the scent. Eventually she came across one of the most beautiful waterfalls she had ever seen. The water was crystal blue and the bushes and trees were a majestic green. Her eyes instantly fell onto the path that went behind the waterfall. She hurriedly ran to the path.

The ordeal

This path seemed to go on for longer than she imagined. Suddenly a bright light surrounded her. Ariel began to feel fear, a familiar fear. It was a type of fear she had felt many years ago. She turned around to see the evil old wizard who had hurt her so many years ago. He seemed even more menacing this time. He had a gruesome smile on his face as he said to her, "You thought I was done with you but you knew I would be back. I have taken so many things from you but now I will take everything else. You cannot escape me!" Ariel fell to her knees petrified by the appearance of the wizard. She began to feel faint.

Reward

Suddenly Ariel noticed a small, glowing rock near her knee. On the rock was an inscription that read, "Evil only grows when you resist feeling the fear. Once you accept you are afraid, the evil one's power will diminish." Suddenly the older woman's words came back to Ariel again: "The secret to being successful in your journey is to accept your fear while you are in the forest. When you accept your fear you will have great magic." Ariel felt the only thing she could do at this point was to give in to what the older woman had instructed her to do. With every step closer of the evil wizard Ariel allowed herself to feel all the fear even when it made her body shake. Even though she did not know if she would survive, Ariel allowed herself to feel all her fear. She looked him right in the eye and yelled at him, "I'm scared!"

The road back

The evil old wizard stopped moving towards her. He began to tremble. Ariel noticed her fear beginning to move through her and into the wizard. For some magical reason, because she allowed herself to feel the fear it moved through her and straight into the wizard. He began to move back rapidly. The more she allowed herself to feel, the faster it moved through her. Finally the wizard was overcome with fear. He jumped back screaming for her to make it stop. He began to cry and scream in agony.

Resurrection

Part of Ariel wanted this evil old wizard to suffer for what he had done but another part of her knew what he was feeling as she had been enduring fear like this for so many years. He screamed and begged to be set free from his torment. Ariel felt all the hatred of the wizard begin to diminish as she saw how much he suffered. She spoke out to him, "If I release you will you return to where you came from and bother me no more?" "Yes! Yes!" screamed the wizard. "Very well then, you are now free." Instantly the wizard felt the fear vanish. He stood up, waved his wand and disappeared. A feeling of peace came over Ariel.

Ariel picked up the rock with the inscription. She walked out from behind the waterfall and instantly noticed how different the forest looked. Previously it was dark and scary but now it was light and peaceful. She began her walk home with her magic rock. She noticed how differently the forest felt to her than when she began her journey.

Return

After a very long but pleasant walk Ariel came out of the forest near her small home. She was exhausted but felt more alive than she had in many years. She reached the wooden chair in her garden and sat down. She wondered how all the amazing things that happened to her came to be. In that moment she heard a familiar voice behind her: "It came to be because I needed it to be." Ariel turned around to see the older woman standing behind her. In that moment she realised that this woman was not only a woman of great magical ability; she realised the older woman was herself. "That is true," said the woman, who seemed to read Ariel's thoughts. "I needed you to discover the magic to heal so that I can help others to heal." And in a flash she was gone.

This kind of mythic story is something that I would rarely use with adult clients but the opportunity to tell Lori a story "for her child" enabled me to give a directive in how to deal with anxiety to her unconscious mind through the guise of a harmless story to help her child sleep. Using mythic-tinged stories like this can be very helpful when working with children. The format of the hero's journey can be used without an elaborate magical setting. Here is an example from a session with a client in recovery after a history of substance abuse. This client was fearful of falling back into old patterns of use. The story told has the same qualities of the hero's journey yet it is an everyday situation. The story told to the client was about another person's journey of recovery:

The ordinary world
Joe had been drinking heavily for a couple of years. When he started drinking he had enjoyed the effects his drinking gave him but he knew there must be more to life than what he was experiencing. He continued drinking excessively even after he lost contact with his family and lost his job due to his alcohol use. He felt like he was about to hit rock bottom.

The call to adventure
An acquaintance told him about a group of people dealing with addiction issues who met weekly. Part of Joe wanted to seek out this new avenue but he hesitated to face all the things he knew he would confront in dealing with his drinking, such as shame and guilt. He worried whether he could live without his alcohol.

Meeting with the mentor
One day he met an older man who was part of this group and this man told him how the group was not judgmental and really just wanted to help each other recover from the damage addiction had done to them. Joe felt a sense of connection with the older man and agreed to come to the meeting.

Crossing the threshold
It was a scary experience the first time he showed up as he did not know what to expect, but he began to feel comfortable with the people in the group. He started going to the group several times a week. He continued to learn more about addiction and what he could to change his patterns of use.

Test and trials
Joe finally made the commitment to stop drinking alcohol. It was a scary time for him for the next few weeks as he was constantly tempted by every thought and feeling to fall back into his old dysfunctional patterns.

Approach and the ordeal
Unfortunately he started drinking again. He felt so ashamed that he stopped going to his meetings. It was only when he got a call from the older man who invited him to the group that Joe confessed his weakness. The older man told Joe that he was not weak but just needed some more help and understanding to keep working through his problem. Joe started going back to the meetings and worked with a sponsor in the group who was there to help guide and assist him during trying times.

Reward and the road back
He continued making progress and felt better every day.

Resurrection and return

Joe eventually became a sponsor in the meetings and worked to help others overcome their addiction to alcohol. He has been clean and sober for over eight years now and has personally helped many people save themselves from addiction.

Not every story has to have dramatic archetypal qualities in order to invoke inner resources within a client. Everyday events can just as easily (if not more so) assist the client in gaining access to more creative ways of solving problems. Here are some examples of short stories about everyday activities with embedded messages for the client's unconscious:

A parent who is having issues with being too involved in her daughter's life may be supplied with the following story when the therapist learns the client enjoys gardening:

> It is important to make sure the plant gets enough water but not too much water. It can be an interesting problem. We want the plant to grow strong and resilient so we need to help it by making sure it gets enough nutrients and water. Without good nutrients and water the plant will dry up and die. However, if we overwater the plant we run the risk of keeping it from becoming resilient. In some cases it is important for the plant to go without water for short periods of time as it makes the plant more attuned to the environment and draw on its own water reserves to stay alive. If we continue to water the plant even when it doesn't need it we can keep the plant from reaching its potential, and it can remain very weak and its root structure can eventually rot.

An insecure client who is apprehensive about making new friends can be told a story about how children are often resistant to eating new foods:

> You know how children can be so picky about eating the same things all the time? They only want to experience one or maybe two types of food. There could be so many other delicious meals they could eat but these children only want to stick to eating what they know and have previously experienced. It is as if they

are afraid of the unknown taste of the food. I have seen several children who would not even eat tasty junk food like pizza or hamburgers because they are resistant to trying something different. They worry about whether the new food will taste as good as what they are already eating. It is as if they spend so much time worrying about whether the new food will taste good or not that they cheat themselves out of the possibility of eating something absolutely delicious. But, as you know, not everything children try to eat will taste good but if they try enough foods they find that the majority of the things they eat will be delicious. This will also give them a way out of the boring mundane diet of only one or two foods to enjoy. The larger the variety of foods to be tried ensures more positive experiences.

Using the interspersal technique with stories

When telling stories Erickson was fond of using what he referred to as the "interspersal technique". This technique is used for indirectly delivering suggestions to clients while discussing topics other than the subject of the suggestions. Erickson would distinguish certain phrases in his sentences using different vocal tones and volume. This can be a powerful method of indirectly moving a client into a different view of the presenting problem (Erickson, Rossi, & Rossi, 1976).

These hidden suggestions are a great way to work with resistant clients who dismiss any outright directives offered by the therapist. The interspersal technique can allow the therapist to supply information to the client at the unconscious level by bypassing the resistant client's conscious dismissiveness. This also allows the client to unconsciously respond to the suggestion without consciously being seen as accepting directives or losing perceived power or control. This technique usually works best embedded in a story that contains something of interest to the client. This ensures full conscious attention on the topic, which allows the client's unconscious mind to become open to the therapist's suggestions (Erickson, 1966).

I have found that a very slight pause before and after the phrase I want the client's unconscious to receive is the easiest way for me to deliver the interspersal technique. Dolan (1985) wisely points out therapists want to avoid raising their voices when delivering suggestions.

It may be best to slightly lower the inflection of the voice when deliver the unconscious messages as it will draw less conscious attention from the client. I have italicised the suggestions I want the client's unconscious to accept.

For example, when working with a client who is overly anxious about making mistakes in life, the therapist could tell a story about an artist working on a painting:

> When an artist is painting, he really has to *become open to what will happen in the moment.* If there is too much concern with getting everything perfect it will cause undue stress and prevent the painting from being completed. I had a friend who wanted to learn to be an artist. He took many classes to learn the techniques and seemed to be a natural at painting. However, his teacher kept telling him, *"You have to relax and just let things happen."* She told him this because he was far too worried about what the finished product would look like. She told him he needed to *allow things to happen all on their own.* She felt that when he didn't get something just right it was *a way to have new experiences and opportunities for growth.* He worked really hard to get into a state of relaxation and *let go of all worries about whether things will be good or bad* but the secret was he did not need to work hard at it. When a person is able to *let go of all expectations* he can find such enjoyment when painting. If at the end of the painting session the picture did not come out the way the artist had wished, he simply moves on to the next painting.

When working with a client who feels stuck after the dissolving of a relationship:

> Mechanics can do wonders when working on cars. They know just by the sound of the engine if a vehicle needs to *continue moving forward* or not. Sometimes I hear mechanics talking about how people really *enjoy seeing new things and having new experiences* in their cars. They talk about how many people *feel a sense of openness and relaxation* when driving on the open road. It is nice to know the road ahead offers drivers *new opportunities to discover new things.* Sometimes it is much better than taking the bus or the subway. *You can have freedom* to take whatever route you wish.

Therapeutic tasks

Often intellectual insight will do little to change a person's emotions or behaviour yet a physical experience can assist a client in becoming more flexible in how he deals with a specific problem or situation. Therapeutic tasks are constructed and assigned for the purpose of representing the client's problem (as well as the solution) in a symbolic but indirect manner to the client's unconscious mind. These tasks can incorporate any action, situation, or item. The goal is to use the assignment to express the problem and subsequent solution in a tangible way for the client. What is nice about assigning a task to a client is that he can experience the therapeutic process outside the therapy room, which allows the client to integrate healing experiences in a way that is unique to him.

When asking a client to perform an action, we as therapists need to be aware that there is always a potential for the client to refuse. At no time should we appear to be forcing a client to do something. This defeats the purpose of assigning a task. If a client refuses to perform a task it is usually due to lack of rapport between therapist and client, the client being overwhelmed by what is being asked or not viewing the task as something significant to him. We can usually avoid many of the clashes with clients over the assignment of tasks by maintaining trust and rapport in the therapeutic relationship. If our client knows we have their best interests at heart he will usually follow our directives.

Erickson often used tasks and rituals as a way to supply the client with resources to help overcome a problem that in-depth discussion may not alleviate. Once he worked with a man who was in constant physical discomfort. The man had become motivated to build a house for his wife in spite of his discomfort. He had worked long and hard on the project but as he began to finish the house he became depressed and ceased working on it. He then began spending his days only complaining of his physical pain and sitting in a rocking chair.

Erickson told the man he was to help a couple Erickson knew who needed a flower garden planting. The man was directed to go to the couple's home every day and work in their garden, and then report to Erickson on his progress after the day's work was completed. After working for the couple, the man continued to plant several other flower gardens in town. His depression soon lifted and he returned to work on the house he had been building (Gordon & Meyers-Anderson, 1981).

I once worked with a young woman who needed some coaching on becoming more creative in her work. She felt stuck and limited in what she was presently doing. She told me she had bought several books on creativity but these books had little effect on her being able to unleash her creative spirit. She felt she was becoming slightly depressed due to her frustration and had begun to avoid some aspects of her work she had previously enjoyed. I directed her to take the books on creativity she had bought and arrange them in different ways four times a day. These arrangements could not look the same. The books had to be in totally different arrangements each time. She had free rein on how she was to arrange the books with the only other directive being that she drew a picture of how she arranged the books each time she did it and brought the pictures with her to the next session. Within a week she reported a renewed zest for creativity and began having new, exciting ideas.

Inspired by Erickson's interventions, Haley (1973) described the use of therapeutic ordeals designed to give the client the directive to make the symptom currently experienced so uncomfortable that the client is motivated to cease having it rather than continue with the problem. This is accomplished by linking the occurrence of the problem to another undesired experience. An example of this type of therapeutic task would be the case in which Erickson required a client who had insomnia to stand at his mantelpiece all night reading books that he had been putting off reading. The client's displeasure at having to stand and read less than exciting books eventually led to the client choosing sleep over insomnia (Haley, 1993).

Erickson worked with a seventy-year-old woman whose fifty-year-old son was schizophrenic. She was very bothered by her son's erratic behaviour to the point where she could not go to the library to read, as she had to take her son, who she felt couldn't be left alone, and he would cause her such grief. Her son would constantly follow her around making noises and acting up. Erickson directed her to drive out into the desert near her home, drop off her son, drive three miles towards home, and wait for him to arrive on foot. She had time to read her library book in silence without being bothered by her son's erratic behaviour. Erickson let her know that her son would try to manipulate her by falling or crawling on his walk or by waiting for hours for her to return. He told her she was not to give in but to wait as long as it took for him to arrive on foot. The woman followed Erickson's directions and found she enjoyed the quiet reading time her actions gave her. Her son began to volunteer to walk if his mother drove only one mile away from him instead of three miles. In time his disruptive behaviour started to improve (Haley, 1984).

Once I worked with a man named Ben who professed to be addicted to food. He was well over 350 pounds due to his constant eating of unhealthy food. His wife was frustrated with his ceaseless eating of junk food and sweets. She was concerned about his weight and angry he did not listen to her when she asked him to cut back on his intake of food. Ben's pattern for eating was consistent. He would leave for work in the morning and immediately stop at a fast-food restaurant where he bought a very high fat, processed breakfast. He would snack on sweets all through the day at work and for lunch he would return to a fast-food restaurant where he indulged in all he could eat. For dinner he went to restaurants with buffets where he could indulge his burning desire for more high-fat food. At weekends he sat in front of the television or played computer games while he ate sweets and pizza. He rarely ate at home and spent a fair bit of money on his meals every day.

Ben related to me how he was a "stress eater" and he ate this way due to his feeling insecure about his finances. He had an overwhelming fear of poverty even though he and his wife had good jobs with decent incomes. He had a job he did not fully enjoy but was terrified of leaving because the money was good. He told me he worried a good deal about not having enough money for his retirement and feared losing his job, which could result in losing his home. He reaffirmed to me it was this stress that was responsible for his declining health and excessive weight.

Ben believed he could not control his addiction as he felt it was a compulsion and he was helpless to stop it. He also told me up front he had little desire to stop his unhealthy eating, as it was one of his few pleasures in life. I told him he need not stop eating bad food. He was instead to continue eating the way he had been but he now had a task to perform when he enjoyed his food. I directed Ben to obtain a receipt for every junk food purchase he made and present it to his wife at the end of the week. He then was to write her a cheque for the same amount he spent on junk food that week. She was to do what she wanted to with the money as long as she spent it on something frivolous. He was to keep a tally of how much the food and the cheques to his wife totalled at the end of the month.

After two weeks Ben began to see how much money he was spending, not just on his food, but also the money he had to give to his wife. He began to become anxious about his financial security. If he ate more food when he was anxious he would essentially be hurting himself financially so he decided he would only change his breakfast routine. He decided to eat before he left the house for work. His wife only bought healthy foods so he decided to suffer through a healthy meal in the morning. After a week of his eating breakfast at home, he saw his check to his wife become smaller so he thought maybe he could cut back on eating out at lunch and instead bring something from home. He also noticed how his trousers were a little looser and more comfortable. Encouraged by his progress, he even signed up to ride the exercise bike at the gym at work.

Over time Ben decided to put the money he had been spending on junk food and cheques to his wife into a savings account that steadily grew as his waistline shrunk. He still ate junk food a few times a week but nowhere near as much as before. He also began to relax about his financial future as he watched his savings account increase every week. He continued to ride the exercise bike at the gym and found he enjoyed the results working out gave him.

Therapeutic rituals

The term "ritual" can bring to mind many different images and preconceptions. Rituals are powerful actions that are all around us in both religious and secular settings. One can consider standing for the national anthem as a ritual. Having a funeral after a loved one dies is a ritual. Weddings and graduation ceremonies can be considered rituals.

According to many researchers the use of rituals is designed to cause a shift in one's consciousness. It is a method of opening up to other ways of being in the world. The great mythologist Joseph Campbell believed that rituals could put one in direct touch with mythic reality. Rituals can, if done correctly, be powerful methods of setting intention in life. Rituals can also be used to facilitate healing, mark important transitions in emotional development, and signal new beginnings in life's journey.

From the psychotherapy perspective rituals can be very effective at assisting individuals (and families) in creating new patterns of responding to and interacting with the environment. Often, people feel stuck in a certain pattern and are not sure how to change it. In his book *Rituals in Psychotherapy: Transition and Continuity* (1983), Onno Van Der Hart writes that he feels the use of rituals to work through significant psychological distresses can result in major shifts in cognitions and emotional patterns, and that rituals can create the process of healing in a manner that few other interventions can demonstrate.

Case studies from the field of family therapy are full of examples of therapists giving clients odd rituals to perform that indirectly create a change in the patterns the family exhibited. In other cases families may need to hold on to their rituals during difficult times to ensure and strengthen their connection to each other. I remember reading an article that stressed the importance of the family dinner as a ritual in preserving the emotional health of the family. In our world today many of our everyday rituals are disappearing, which may account for so many people feeling disconnected from others and the world around them.

When a therapist gives a client a ritual to perform it is often geared towards giving the client more flexibility and resources in working through the present issue being faced. If clients feel stuck, they merely lack the experience of a new action to take. Once the action has been taken in the form of a ritual, clients will know (at the unconscious level) that they have more options than previously considered. These rituals can be created to assist clients in making major life transitions in such areas as relationships, work, and aging. Using odd rituals in therapy may sound a little silly to our linear thinking, conscious mind but to our unconscious it can act as a gateway to new healing experiences.

For example, I worked with a client named Walter who was seeking therapy due to an upcoming divorce. His wife had a consistent pattern of infidelity and seemed to have no desire to reform and become monogamous in their marriage. Walter was hurt and depressed by his wife's actions and was worried about the effect this situation was going to have on his young daughter. He had been separated from his wife for a couple of months. Even though he felt divorce was the right thing to do in this situation, he was totally stuck in moving forward with his life. He really felt he loved his soon to be ex-wife and had trouble imagining a life without her. He could not even bring himself to begin getting rid of some of the things that belonged to his wife that she had left behind at his home. Seeing those items and not having a vision of a life without her led to his feeling more depression and heartache.

After we covered the important points of what brought him to therapy, I knew it was going to be difficult for him to begin the process of becoming more disengaged from his wife. Rather than directly putting forth a plan to begin moving him away from his old relationship, I decided to enact a ritual to help Walter move forward. I asked him if he would be interested in doing a small action that could help him feel better. He said he was very interested. I told him that what I was going to ask him to do may seem a little strange but it was in his best interest. His curiosity was aroused but he was a little apprehensive about what I would say. He let me know he was still open to what I was going to recommend.

I sat quietly for a moment. I then looked him directly in the eyes with some intensity and told him I thought he needed to perform an exorcism. This statement was not what he had expected to hear. "An exorcism?" he asked, to make sure he had heard me correctly. "Yes, you need to exorcise a room in your house." At this point he was surprised and amused. "I think you have a real issue that needs a different approach. The exorcism you will perform is not for ridding your home of the devil but rather the pain of this relationship. I want you to take all of your wife's belongings out of one room in your house. Put these in the garage for three days. After you take her things out of the room I want you to get yourself some incense from your local store. Choose the kind that you like the best. Light the incense and face each wall of the room where you removed her belongings and make the sign of the cross (this client was a devout Christian). After you make the sign of the cross say out loud four times, 'I ask for peace and love in the name of the Father.' Do this ritual seven times each day for three days. After three days you can feel free to bring in your wife's belongings and put them back in the room."

Walter did not expect to hear this kind of assignment from a psychotherapist. In spite of him being surprised by my odd directions, a part of him appeared to be excited and energised to begin this assignment. I was not telling him to get rid of his soon to be ex-wife's belongings but rather just to put them somewhere else for a few days. This action gave him the flexibility and experience of moving her things to the garage, which could possibly lead to eventually moving the items out of the home. Making the sign of the cross invoked within him a feeling of connection with his religion, which previously had given him comfort when life was tough.

At our next session Walter reported he had performed the ritual as directed. He said he had a new sense of possibility about the future. He now had a feeling of hope that even though he was very sad, he could go on and create a new future with someone who would be faithful to him. He was now more focused on ensuring his young daughter would be cared for and that the two of them could begin to create a new future as a family.

I certainly could have spent our time together working on Walter's illogical beliefs about the future, the family issues that brought him to therapy, or his self-esteem troubles, but I felt that a ritual would do more to begin the healing process within him. The action I directed him to take was so different from what he had been doing that he had no choice but to have a new experience. His practice of taking charge of moving things in his house and asking for help from his God gave him the necessary resources he needed to create new changes in his patterns.

The goal for using rituals in psychotherapy is for the clients to have an experience that supplies them with a resource to create a change in their situation. Clients come to therapy because they believe there is a problem beyond their ability to solve on their own. To me, this means clients feel they do not have the necessary resources to cope effectively and transcend a situation labelled by them as a "problem". If by performing a specific set of actions clients are given the needed resources (or reminded of the resources they already possess), they can begin to solve their own problems. This in turn helps to increase their sense of control and self-efficacy in their lives.

Often rituals can be constructed based on what the therapist hears in the unconscious metaphors and analogies the client uses. The words a client chooses can reveal a tremendous amount about how she views her world. By paying attention to frequently occurring patterns in a client's speech, a therapist can gain an enormous amount of information on what resources the client needs to access.

For example, an older man named Gary came to therapy complaining of feeling depressed. He had lost his wife the previous year and had recently moved into a new retirement neighbourhood. He told me he did not feel at home in his new house and neighbourhood yet. He was sleeping more than usual and starting to avoid interacting with others. He rarely did much more than stay inside his home, watch the news on, and read mystery books.

In our session Gary said: "You know, I just feel like a fish out of water here. I don't know if I fit in. It has been a struggle to move in and get to know the other people in the neighbourhood. I am afraid that I am a little different to many of the people here. I don't want to come into a new community and rock the boat too much. There is a lot to do in getting set up in a new place and it can be overwhelming to me. Sometimes I feel like I am swimming upstream. I don't feel like I can catch a break these days."

One can easily see a metaphor pattern involving the following:

Fish out of water
Rock the boat
Swimming upstream
Catch a break.

The ritual given to him was to go to a special store for fishing enthusiasts, buy a rod and reel, and begin to practise fishing in his backyard for fifteen minutes a day. He could stand on his porch and cast off into the backyard. He needed to have his fishing hat and boots on when he performed this ritual. He could also have his cooler with nice, cold drinks available for him to enjoy. He had to do this every day for two weeks but he could decide what time of day he wanted to backyard fish.

Gary reported back that the practice allowed him some quiet time to reflect on some of the emotional things he had been avoiding which included beginning to let go of some of the grief associated with the death of his wife. He noticed also he had begun to relax more in his new neighbourhood and even invited a new friend he had met to go on a real fishing excursion with him. He began to feel a desire to get to know other people in his neighbourhood and was even considering starting a mystery book club for people in his neighbourhood who shared a similar fondness for mystery fiction.

Another example of designing a ritual based on metaphors involves a woman named Belinda who sought counselling for dealing with the high stress levels associated with her work. Belinda was working in a fast-paced financial services company. In her job she constantly had to juggle many different tasks, which led to more stress than she desired. She worked really hard at her job and hoped to be able to climb the corporate ladder to a better-paid position within the company.

In our session Belinda stated: "I am just so damn knotted up all the time. I am overwhelmed. I desperately want to be able to relax but this job ties me down to such a tight schedule. I am still hoping to advance with this company but lately I am afraid they are stringing me along and the thought of that makes me even more stressed."

The key phrases here are:

Knotted up
Ties me down
Stringing me along.

Belinda had told me exactly what she needed. She needed to be released from the ropes of her stress. Her ritual was based on what she unconsciously told me. She was directed to go to a charity shop in her town and to be on the lookout for an old doll. She was told she would instantly know which doll was the right one when she saw it. She was to purchase the doll, take it home and clean it up from the dust and grime of the shop. She was then to give the doll a name she liked. After this she was to get three different kinds of wool and wrap them tightly around the doll from top to bottom. After she tied up the doll she was to put it in a dark cupboard for eight hours. When she came back to the doll, she was to cut all the tight wool off the doll and place it in a seat of honour at the dining room table for one night (she lived alone so she did not have to explain this odd ritual to anyone).

As ridiculous as this ritual sounds, it had a real effect on Belinda. She returned to the next session and said she had for some strange reason been able to relax and breath easier lately. She ended up working on the doll's dress with material she had left over from another craft project and then gave it to her young niece. She discovered that she enjoyed sewing and found a new hobby to help her stress levels. Belinda no longer felt as tied down to her job and even said she was becoming more open to a possible career change in the future.

Gary and Belinda both needed to gain access to certain resources in order to solve their problems. From the therapist's perspective they already had exactly what was necessary to change but just needed an experiential process to be reminded they already had all the resources necessary for that change to occur. By listening to the underlying messages outside the client's awareness, the therapist can create rituals that may seem odd to the conscious mind but give the unconscious just what it needs to heal. It is important for therapists to ask themselves what ways there are by which clients can move through their trials and tribulations other than just talking with them (although that alone can be pretty powerful). Sometimes our clients need certain actions to shake things up and give themselves the resources and experiences they need to solve their own problems.

CHAPTER FIVE

The Renaissance man

The following is a transcript of a therapy session with seventeen-year-old Stanley, who came to me with his mother seeking help for depression. He was referred for counselling by his medical doctor who had already prescribed antidepressants for Stanley. In addition, a local psychologist had diagnosed Stanley as suffering from major depression and attention deficit hyperactivity disorder. Stanley's mother was a housewife who was busy raising Stanley and his ten-year-old sister. Stanley's father was a medical doctor working close to twelve-hour days in the emergency room of a large hospital. Mother and son appeared to genuinely care for one another and both seemed ready for Stanley to begin feeling better as soon as possible.

S = Stanley
M = Mother
T = Therapist

T: Okay, so what motivated you to come to see me today?
s: I have been depressed.
T: For how long?
s: For over two years.

T: Two years is a long time.

S: Yeah, it has been a long time.

T: How do you know you're depressed?

S: I just feel really sad.

T: Is there a specific thing you are feeling sad about?

S: No, I don't know why I am feeling sad. It just kind of happens.

T: What else do you do when you are depressed?

S: I don't know. I just don't feel like doing much.

T: I see. Now, if I had to be you and feel, think, and see the things you do when you are depressed what would I have to experience?

(It is important to pin down this pattern of depression by asking the client to give a detailed breakdown of how the pattern is created and maintained.)

S: I don't understand.

T: Okay, no worries. What I mean is, if you had to teach me to feel the way you do, which you label "depressed", what would I need to feel?

S: Oh, I guess you would need to feel sad and …

T: So how would I need to feel sad?

(These questions are causing Stanley to shift uncomfortably in his seat, as it may be that he has not previously really examined the feelings he is experiencing. The continued examination of his emotional state is an attempt to get Stanley to be very specific about the pattern he has been creating. It is usually unwise to begin changing patterns without a clear representation of all the elements that play a part.)

S: Oh, I don't know. I guess I have to feel that nothing matters.

T: Nothing matters? Okay, is there anything that could matter during this time?

S: No, not really. I just kind of feel like there is no point in anything.

T: Okay, I think I understand. Mum, does this sound familiar to you?

M: Yes, he has told me that he feels empty and that there is nothing that really matters to him when he is depressed. He also will just stay in his room all alone and either lie in his bed or play his guitar.

T: Oh, cool! So you are a musician, huh?

s: Yeah, I try.

t: How long have you been playing?

s: A little over two years. I am still not as good as I would like to be.

t: I am sure you are pretty good at what you do. What kind of music do you play?

s: Mostly rock but also some blues.

t: Some blues? How much do you enjoy playing the blues?

s: I enjoy it. It is fun.

t: So you are being helped to understand the soul of the blues by this depression. I noticed you started feeling depressed about two years ago and you started playing the guitar over two years ago.

s: Huh. I don't know. I hadn't thought about it like that.

t: Yeah. It could be that the depression helped you to get in touch with how to be an authentic bluesman.

(By pointing out how being depressed may have helped him in some small way, Stanley's symptoms are being reframed to be more than just a meaningless experience.)

s: Maybe. I still don't like it.

t: Who would? Depression is not supposed to be fun. The old blues singers didn't sing songs about how much fun, wealth, or great relationships they had, did they?

s: (smiling) No.

t: Maybe I'm wrong but it seems like to be able to really play the blues one might have to have experienced some depression at some point in one's life.

s: Maybe.

t: Do you write any blues songs?

s: Kind of, they are more rock but sound bluesy.

t: Nice. Do you play in a band?

s: I used to have a group of guys come over and play but we don't jam together anymore.

t: Why not?

s: They got busy with jobs and girlfriends. Things like that.

m: They were pretty good.

t: You heard them play?

m: Yes, they would come to the house and I would hear them practising.

T: So you don't jam with anyone these days?

S: No, not too much.

T: Do you ever bring out your guitar and play a song for Mum?

S: Sometimes.

M: He hasn't in a while.

T: Have you ever thought about writing a song about the depression?

S: About the depression?

T: Yes, about your experience of being depressed.

S: I have never thought about it. I usually just write music.

T: So no lyrics?

S: Some but I'm not a great singer so I don't sing the lyrics.

T: I'm wondering if you could write me a song about the depression and bring it with you to your next session.

S: I don't know, I guess I could. That would be different.

T: Would you be comfortable bringing your guitar in here and playing it for me?

S: Sure. I have an acoustic guitar I could bring.

T: Excellent! I look forward to a free concert. Oh, and you got to play something from your second album, okay?

S: (laughs).

T: Okay. Cool. So what else are you doing to feel depressed? I have already heard you are staying in your room and feeling like nothing matters.

S: Yeah. I guess I just want to get away from the feelings. I sometimes sneak off and smoke some pot or I drink.

T: [To Stanley's mother] Is this news to you or were you already aware about this?

M: We knew he was smoking pot and drinking.

T: How did you respond to finding this out?

M: We grounded him. He couldn't go anywhere for a while. We also locked up the little bit of alcohol we have in the house in a safe.

S: Yeah, I was able to get the alcohol out of the safe.

T: Was the safe locked?

S: Yeah, it wasn't that hard.

M: I had no idea you had got into the alcohol in the safe! I am surprised.

(At this point Stanley's mother appears to be a little upset as her eyes begin to moisten).

T: So this is the first time you heard about this, huh?

M: Yes … I am really worried about Stanley. He feels so bad and he has been drinking, and doing drugs. We just don't know what to do any more. We want to trust that he will be Okay but then I come in here and find out he has opened the safe. It is tough because I can't watch him all the time and his father is usually gone during most of the day so sometimes no one is at home with him.

T: Yeah, breaking into the safe is a surprise. Where is Dad during most of the day?

M: He is an emergency room doctor. He has to drive almost an hour to get to the hospital and then he is there for close to twelve hours a day. He isn't home much these days.

T: I know medical doctors work a lot of hours but you are saying he is working more than he has in the past?

M: Yes, plus the driving time.

T: When did Dad start working so many more hours?

M: About two years ago.

S: I'm sorry about the safe, Mum.

(There is a brief silence as Stanley's mother composes herself and Stanley looks down at the floor appearing slightly ashamed).

T: You know, a couple of things came to my mind just a second ago. First, Dad started being away from home more often about two years ago and it was two years ago that Stanley started feeling depressed.

M: Hmm … I hadn't thought about that.

T: [to Stanley] And second and more importantly, I can't help thinking about how you got into the locked safe. How did you do that? I would have absolutely no clue how to crack a safe. Mum, it is not easy to do that. Stanley must be very bright and capable to figure that out. I have trouble unlocking my office when I have keys in my hand so I can't even imagine trying to get into a locked safe.

M: He is very smart. He used to get really good grades before he started feeling depressed.

(At this point, an effort is made to continue to move the mother away from too much focus on Stanley's depression. In order to create a shift in the interaction patterns of the family dealing with Stanley's depression, the focus of the session needs to be on Stanley's resource: his intelligence and talent.)

T: Yeah, you know it takes some real ingenuity to crack a safe. Stanley, did you have to use a stethoscope like in the movies? Did you swipe one from your dad?

S: No. It really isn't hard.

T: I just have this mental image of you dressed in black, wearing dark sunglasses, with a stethoscope placed on the safe slowly turning the knob until you hear it click and then cracking it open.

S: [laughs] No, it wasn't like that.

T: You could be in that movie about the guys who do that huge heist in Las Vegas. You need a cool nickname like other nefarious individuals have in that line of work. Maybe you could go by "Stanley the Cracker"?

M: [laughs] I can't picture him as a safe cracker.

S: [smiling] Me neither.

T: "Stanley the safe-cracking bluesman"? You could play blues songs as you crack the safe.

S: I think I would like another line of work rather than that.

T: I hear you. What if instead of that depression song you were going to write me you wrote me a song about depressed safe-cracking bluesmen instead?

[Everyone laughs]

S: I think the song about depression would be easier to do.

T: You are probably right.

S: I only broke into the safe because I felt so depressed that I wanted to feel different. The same with pot. I only smoke when I am feeling really depressed. It is not like I am addicted to anything, you know.

T: How much do you know about the effects of marijuana?

S: A good bit. I read on the internet about all the possible negative effects and how sometimes pot can get laced with some other drugs that can be very dangerous. I made sure that the pot I smoked was from someone I knew and trusted, as I didn't want to have any problems.

T: Wow, you really took the time to look all that stuff up before you started using marijuana?

S: Yeah, I really haven't used it that much. I only really want to do it when I am having a bad day feeling depressed.

T: Where specifically did you research the information about pot?

S: I read some articles on the internet. The articles were written by some scientists for a journal. I don't know which one but it had a lot of chemistry in it.

T: Wow! [To the mother] Did you hear how thorough Stanley was in investigating drugs before he started using? I wish more young people would find out about the harmful effects of the different drugs before they blindly started using them. [To Stanley] I mean you even went to some elite scientific journals. That is really unique. So many people would not even remotely be interested in researching in depth those kinds of things. You are really a smart guy.

M: Yes, he can be very smart. I don't know what to do about the alcohol in the house if he is clever enough to get into the safe.

T: You could take it over to a friend's house unless you and your husband feel you need to have it at the house.

(This is an indirect question to find out if alcohol is a problem for the mother and the father.)

M: Yeah, I guess we could although there isn't much alcohol. We just have a couple of bottles of wine and some bourbon. I guess I could give that to someone I know.

T: Sure. [To Stanley] Is that the only place you get your alcohol?

S: At this point, yeah. I don't really go anywhere any more other than school so I guess ... yeah that is the only place.

T: What about the pot?

S: You mean, where do I get it?

T: Yes.

S: I got it from a former friend of mine but I don't see him too much anymore.

T: How many friends do you see?

S: I see some people at school but only really Adam after school.

T: Adam?

S: Yeah.

T: How long have you known him?

S: Over three years. He also plays music.

T: Does he drink or do pot?

s: No, he actually goes to church and is very serious about his schoolwork.

t: [playfully] Well, why the heck are you hanging around that guy?

s: [laughing] I don't know. He is really cool. He has been playing on this rugby team. He asked me if I wanted to join.

t: Does that interest you?

s: Yeah. I don't know why but I think it would be fun to do.

(Stanley has now presented a resource to aid in changing his pattern. Playing rugby is a physical activity that Stanley has not up to now been engaging in as he lies in his bed feeling depressed. Playing rugby also entails interacting with other team members. According to Stanley, he does not interact with others too often and socialisation with team mates could break the pattern of isolation he has been performing.)

t: Wow. Rugby, huh? That is a unique sport around here isn't it?

s: Yeah.

t: Mum, how do you feel about Stanley playing rugby? It can be a very demanding sport.

m: Oh, I think it would be great if he had a new hobby.

t: Me too. [To Stanley] What do you like about rugby?

s: Well, it seems like a lot of fun. It is so different from the other sports around here. Everyone I know plays baseball, soccer, or football. I have never cared about playing those sports. The guys I have met who play it are really cool.

(At this point Stanley is becoming fairly animated as he talks about the possibility of playing rugby.)

t: Yeah, it is a fairly unique sport around here. What else is interesting about it to you?

(Stressing how rugby is a unique sport is a way to activate a resource of a feeling of significance in Stanley. He has already commented on how he feels nothing matters, so experiencing a new activity he desires to do as unique and significant may counteract some of his previous experience of feeling meaningless.)

S: I guess it would be the guys aren't all padded up. It seems like it can get a bit rough but every game I have watched all the guys seem to be having a great time and get along.

T: It is a physical game isn't it?

S: Yeah.

T: And I would think it would be a lot of work, wouldn't it?

S: Yeah.

T: You would have to work well with your team in order to win.

S: Sure. The guys on the team seem really cool and work together well.

T: That's good. I think sports can be a great way to excel in many areas of one's life. I remember reading an article about a famous athlete— I don't remember his name—and in this article he said it is really important to work with a good team … if you want to succeed as an individual player. What he meant by this is … there are times when he felt like he couldn't do more than he was doing … but he knew the team was depending on him … so it motivated him to do more than he thought he could. And in the article he had stated there were times that he felt he just couldn't get up … after being knocked down in the game. He truly felt like he wanted to lie there and not move … because he could not find the motivation to get back up. It can be tough … to feel like that. He felt tired and didn't even know if the team was going to win the game or not. He said he felt totally depressed about the score and he felt like at that point … nothing mattered about the game, he felt it was pointless. He just wanted to hide and continue lying down.

(The story of the athlete is a metaphor in which Stanley's previous symptoms of feeling sadness and meaningless and lying on his bed are addressed. The role of a team in a person's life is an important metaphor for moving Stanley out of his old patterns. He has been isolated with limited connection to even his own family lately. His team has dwindled due to his isolation. He has lost interactions with his valuable team members: his mother and sister, his friends from school, his former band mates, and his father. This story is being used as a way to indirectly give him another option for dealing with his depression. He might feel better being a part of a team with a shared goal, whether it is a rugby team, music team, or family team. A player can't win a game if the team members don't interact with one another. If Stanley were to be directly told he needs to increase his interactions with his parents and friends, he may be resistant to taking the directive. With the directive being intertwined within a story about an athlete and his team, Stanley can receive the message at the unconscious level and act on it without any need for conscious resistance on his part.)

T: But he said down deep he knew that if he didn't get up … and get back in the game he would not be supporting the team. The team depended on him … to do more than he felt like doing … even when he didn't feel like doing it … because as he said … if you are going to play in a team you can't just quit and lie down, right?

S: No.

T: Yeah … he said … he had to find a new way to motivate himself to do something different … because it is only when someone does something different that he will get a different result, right?

S: Yeah.

T: So he then realised that interacting with his team gave him the energy in those hard times … those difficult times … to get up and push forward … and the more he interacted with the team the better he felt about his role in the game. He felt it was really all about … getting curious about what new things could happen with the help of the others on the team that really allowed him to … become open to new possibilities … and new opportunities … that helped in changing the way he used to think. He said he felt playing on that team was a major reason he was able to … do more things than he thought he could … and have more success in life. It was not just about winning but about connecting with his teammates for a common goal. So after hearing that I thought playing a sport really can help a person learn to do many new things.

(Stanley is silent for a moment as he processes the story at the unconscious level.)

T: I thought it was kind of a cool story.

S: Yeah.

T: When do you think you will want to start playing rugby?

S: I need to talk to Adam first … to see about what I need to do.

T: When do you think you will talk to him?

s: I guess we could call tonight or tomorrow.

t: Do you have his number on you?

s: It is in my phone.

t: [To mother] I want you guys to call Adam immediately after you leave this office. This is so important. I want Stanley to get started playing this game as soon as possible.

m: [surprised] Okay.

t: Doctor's orders, okay?

m: Okay.

t: I guess you guys are used to having doctor's orders at home with Dad, huh?

m: [laughs] Yes.

(Letting clients leave the office without feeling the necessity of changing their patterns is not a good thing. Stanley's joining the rugby team is very important, as it will be the fastest and easiest change to implement in the pattern.)

t: Are you really up for playing rugby?

s: Sure!

t: You know it will be a tough game, right?

s: Yeah.

t: And you know you may get a little banged up, right?

s: Yeah. I'm okay with that.

(The use of questions with the end of the sentence containing "right?" is an indirect way to obtain verbal agreement for performing the new task.)

t: Good. I think you will make an excellent player. What other things are you interested in other than music, rugby, and safe cracking?

s: (laughs) I don't know ... I really enjoyed learning about history.

t: What type of history?

s: Probably ancient history the most.

t: By ancient history what do you mean?

s: Like ... you know ... Greek, Roman ... that kind of thing.

t: Really?

s: Yeah.

t: I am so surprised.

s: Why?

T: Not too many younger people seem interested in history to begin with and very few have the motivation and intelligence to enter into the study of ancient history …

s: Yeah.

T: … because there is so much to learn about other cultures.

s: Yeah.

T: Are you just interested in Greco-Roman history?

s: No, I like to learn about most ancient cultures.

T: That is so interesting. [To mother] Do you like history as well?

M: I enjoy learning about it but I don't know if I am as interested in it as Stanley.

T: Wow. I just had a major insight Do you know what this family needs to do?

M: What?

T: I want the whole family to go on an archaeological dig.

s: Seriously?

T   Seriously. How do you feel about doing that?

M: I had never thought about doing something like that.

s: Me neither. That sounds cool.

T: Yes and you could do it without leaving the country.

M: All of us?

T: Why not?

M: I mean it is okay for all of us to go.

T: Absolutely. It could even be a nice weekend getaway. You've got to pick a weekend that Dad has off. I think you should all go as soon as possible.

M: That does sound different.

T: [To Stanley] How about you?

s: I think it sounds cool. I wonder where, though …

T: Since you are so good at researching and you already have the interest and knowledge of ancient cultures, I want you to find out some places you could go for a weekend archaeology getaway.

s: Okay.

T: Do you think Dad would be up for this?

M: Sure. He likes to do different things.

s: I think he would be.

T: I read on your intake form you had a ten-year-old daughter. Do you think she would be up for this?

M: She would probably like it. She loves to be outside.
T: And she will get to dig in the dirt.
M: Yep.
T: And it will be okay to get totally dirty this time.
M: [laughs] She will love that.

(The rebuilding of Stanley's family "team" is started with an out of the ordinary family event in which all members will work together. The archaeological dig is an exotic event that the whole family may be intrigued enough to participate in without any resistance. By having the entire family work together at an archaeological site it will create another break in Stanley's pattern of isolation.)

T: So we are all on board to make this happen, right?
M: Sure. It does sound fun.
S: Yeah ... I think it will be cool to do that.
T: Not too many younger people will ever do that kind of thing, you know.
S: Yeah. [smiling]
T: I wish more young people had your interests and abilities.
S: Thanks.
T: Wow ... you know what just occurred to me? [To mother] This guy [pointing at Stanley] is very unique, you know?
M: Yes.
T: What I mean is ... how do I put this ... I think he is a Renaissance man. You guys know what that means, right?

[Both nod]

T: He can do so many things well and he is interested in so many diverse topics. I mean ... I have been joking with him about all the different things he does but now I see a different picture. He is a Renaissance man. He is an artist ... you know, because of the music. He is a researcher. I mean how many young people would look up research journals to learn about the effects of marijuana? He is really into learning so many things. I have been kidding about the safe cracking stuff, but you know what? The fact that he can learn to do that is remarkable. He has some inner drive to learn and do things. He is also going to be an athlete with the rugby and an archaeologist with all the history stuff.

M: I see.

T: Maybe one of the reasons he is depressed is he isn't able to expand his talents as he should. [To Stanley] You are one of those guys who are well on their way to having all these great stories about all they have done in their life.

(Now the depression Stanley has been feeling is reframed from something terrible that "just happens" to him into a signal that Stanley is not getting enough opportunity to grow into a Renaissance man. The focus of the therapy session has shifted from "Stanley the depressed adolescent" to "Stanley the Renaissance man". The focus is now on the resources Stanley naturally has rather than what he feels is missing in his life. By pursuing the life of a "Renaissance man" Stanley will have to do more things he enjoys and interact with more people who have similar interests.)

T: This may not make sense to you two but I see it clearly.

M: No, it makes sense. He has always been really bright and curious about things.

(By making the statement that what was previously said might not make sense to Stanley's mother, it indirectly gets her to validate the suggestions of Stanley being a Renaissance man.)

T: And you certainly must have encouraged this curiosity.

M: I did try to give him all kinds of books about the things he was interested in.

T: Yeah, it shows. I can tell you have really helped shape his interests.

(Now the session shifts to building resources in Stanley's mother. It is quite common to have a parent of a child in therapy engage in self-blame regarding the child's issue. It is important for the implementation of the previous directives to ensure Stanley's mother feels she has done a good job by encouraging him to learn different things. The hope is she will continue to encourage him to seek outside interests and connections with others.)

s: Mum always supports the things I am interested in.

t: That is so good. How about Dad?

s: Him too. He is the one that bought me most of my musical equipment.

t: Great. I really feel we need to shift our focus here. I think the problem was you just weren't getting the opportunities you need to expand into the role of a Renaissance man. You know?

s: Yeah.

(Stanley's expressions and body are more alive and engaged at this point, which is clear evidence that the therapy session is heading in the right direction.)

t: Maybe you guys need to go to the bookshop this week and investigate some of the magazines they have about ancient history?

m: Maybe so.

t: I think you could bring sister as well. Mum and sis could go look at other books and leave you to do some research.

s: Sure.

t: And then afterwards you guys could probably grab some dinner. If Dad is home he could come along. I don't want to leave him out.

m: If he is home we could all go.

t: Those magazines may have some information about archaeological digs that you could go to or maybe at least will give you some ideas.

s: Yeah. I like to look at those kinds of things.

t: Cool.

(The family is given another directive that will create another break in Stanley's isolation. Stanley will be more open to going out for an evening if the directive is hidden in the guise of his doing research in something he is interested in.)

t: How are you two feeling right now?

m: I am kind of excited and hopeful.

s: I am just hoping things get better.

t: Sure. Okay, let's go back over what we are supposed to do after you two leave.

s: Call Adam about Rugby.

T: Yes.

S: Go to the bookstore and do some research on history and some places to do archaeology.

T: Yes.

S: I can't think of anything else.

T: I want you to write me that song about depression.

S: Oh, I had forgotten about that!

T: That's okay. Before you bring me any music I want you to play the song for Mum a few times to make sure it is good.

S: Okay.

T: [playfully] I don't want you coming up here and embarrassing yourself with a bad song.

S: [laughs] Right.

T: This place does have standards, you know?

S: Yeah. [laughs]

T: If you want to you could write a song about Renaissance men.

S: That would be interesting.

T: I think I would like to hear that one. I think I would like to hear that one more than the song about depression.

S: Okay.

T: So when are we going to call Adam and get started with Rugby?

S: Today.

T: Excellent! Mum, are you up for some new adventures with the "Renaissance man"?

M: Sure.

T: This session might not have been what you guys expected.

M: Not really but I feel hopeful.

T: I'm glad.

After pursuing the directives laid out in therapy, Stanley did not feel the need to return to therapy.

CHAPTER SIX

The possessed boy who belched

The following is a transcript of a session I had with a family who had been referred to therapy due to their child's behaviour. Eight-year-old Danny began having emotional outbursts and stated he was suffering from depression and having auditory and visual hallucinations. He had been briefly hospitalised due to an overreactive school official who mistook his statements of wishing he were dead as a definite intention to commit suicide. His mother had told his caseworker that Danny was frequently having "mental breakdowns" and "seeing and hearing people" who were not present. Danny's father had been working as a long-distance truck driver who was often absent most of the year but over the last year had lost his licence as a result of a drink-driving conviction and was unable to drive his truck for at least a year. He spent most of his days sitting around the house feeling bored. Danny's mother, who previously had not worked, was now working six to seven days a week, up to twelve hours a day, at a diner to support the family.

M = Mother
F = Father
D = Danny
T = Therapist

T: I read over the file sent by the caseworker but I want to know from you why you are coming to therapy.

M: We are here because of Danny. He has been having all kinds of upset times and he has been very scared. The doctor has him on medication but I am not sure it is working.

T: Okay. Can you define for me what "upset times" are?

M: He gets really freaked out and he starts crying and he is unable to calm down. He will sometimes cry and be upset for over two hours.

T: How often is he upset like this?

M: Every day.

T: Every day?

M: Yeah. As soon as I get home from work he will start feeling really bad and then he will begin to freak out.

T: Tell me what "freak out" looks like?

M: He will start crying and throwing things and he starts yelling at people who I can't see. He is really scared and I just wish I could help him.

T: Of course you do. The fact that all of you are here tells me you are really motivated to change some things at home.

M: Yes. Danny has been on medications but I don't think they are helping.

T: When did this all start happening?

M: It has probably been over a year, maybe more. Danny has often had some fits since he was a baby but not like what is going on now. He and I always got along pretty well. We used to spend a good bit of time just sitting together on the swing on the front porch talking, just me and him.

T: So the two of you are close?

M: Yes. Most of the time it was just me and him as he [pointing to the father] was always working so much. We were more like friends than mother and son. Now I don't get to see him much because of my work and when I do see him he is often having these issues. It has been kind of hard for us.

T: I'm sure it has.

M: Yeah … things have been bad for probably over a year now.

T: That is a long time.

M: It is.

T: Let me ask you a little more about these upset times … are you sure it happens every night when you come home?

(At this point exceptions to when Danny is having an upset time are being sought. If by chance there is a time when Danny is not feeling upset we need to capitalise on it by finding out what resources are available to not be upset. Too often people generalise problems to the point where they can only see the problem as a constant in their lives instead of periods where the problem is either not there or is not as prevalent in their life.)

M: Yes. It isn't too long after I get home from work. I work close to seven days a week at a diner and by the time I get home I am exhausted. As soon as I walk in he is having all these things happen to him. It takes me close to two hours a night to get him to calm down.

T: That is a long time to have to calm someone down.

M: Yes it is.

T: What are you doing to help him calm down?

M: I hold him and try to talk to him when he is upset. To be honest, he frightens me sometimes when he starts getting scared by things I can't see.

T: Does this help him?

M: A bit but he still has these episodes.

T: Okay. Are you doing all this work of calming Danny by yourself? [To Danny's father] Are you helping her out with this evening performance?

(Father has been sitting quietly with his arms crossed with minimal eye contact or interaction during our initial greetings and in the session so far.)

F: No, she usually takes care of him when he is like that.

T: Have you tried to help her at all with this situation?

F: I tried to help her a while back but I couldn't do anything with him. It is like he is possessed by something. I tried to get him to calm down but he wouldn't.

T: Okay. So lately it has just been her trying to fix this situation.

F: Yeah.

T: Okay.

M: He tried to help Danny but I just don't think there is anything he could do.

T: Yeah, do you guys think Danny is really possessed?

M: I hope not.

F: No, I think he may just have some kind of problem.

T: [To Danny in a playful tone] Okay, you … we have been talking about you so it's now your turn to tell me about what has been going on.

D: I don't know what to say.

T: No problem. I just want to know if you are possessed or not.

[Danny shrugs]

T: Does that mean you aren't or you don't know?

D: I don't know.

T: That's okay. Just tell me a little bit about these upset times. What is happening when you are having an upset time?

D: I don't know. I just see or hear something and then I feel scared. I get really angry but I don't know what to do.

T: What do you do when you see or hear something?

D: I try to get away from it. I stay around Mum so I won't be alone.

T: I understand. [To mother] Has Danny had this problem at school?

M: Yes. He has been really upset at school and tries to run away sometimes. He also told the teacher he wished he was dead.

T: What about hearing and seeing those things at school?

M: He said he did have a few times but not too much.

T: So he is not having these two-hour upset times at school then?

M: He does get upset and has trouble settling down but not too often does he get to the point where he is freaking out for that long.

T: Oh, that is good news then, isn't it?

M: What is?

T: That he isn't going through these two-hour freak-outs at school. He mostly has them in the evenings at home.

M: Oh, yeah. The school counsellor referred us to social services to get help so it wasn't too good but … yeah, it is good that he is not having all the upset at school.

(It is important to reinforce the idea that Danny can have times where he is not being upset or acting psychotic. This family, particularly the mother, is understandably preoccupied with Danny's problem. In order to alter this pattern of fear and apprehension it is important to create out-of-the-ordinary scenarios where Danny is behaving the exact opposite of how he has been acting, even if the upset times do not decrease. This gives the family further evidence that Danny is capable of more than just scary behaviour.)

T: [To Danny] How are things at school?
D: I don't like it.
T: Why not?
D: I don't feel good there.
T: I see. Where do you usually feel good?
D: I like to be at home.
T: Anywhere else.
D: [thinks for a minute] No.
M: We don't go anywhere too much. He mostly goes to school and stays at home.
T: [To Danny] What do you like to do at home?
D: I like to draw and watch cartoons.
T: Are you a good artist?
D: I don't know.
T: I would like to see some of your artwork. What kind of things do you draw?
M: He draws scary things! The pictures are pretty good for an eight year old but they are scary.
T: Scary how?
M: There are pictures of monsters and demons.
T: So are these good pictures of monsters and demons?
M: Yes, they are pretty good but scary.
T: [To father] What do you think of the pictures?
F: I really haven't looked at too many of them.
T: [To Danny] Have you shown these pictures to your dad?
D: Not really. I showed him one I think.

(At this point it is apparent that there is very little interaction between Danny and his father. From the mother's description her relationship with Danny was rather enmeshed with Danny seeing her as his main source of security. Now that his mother is working a good deal outside the home, Danny may feel his resource for security is gone. His pattern of running to his mother for security is taking on a more dysfunctional process with his outburst episodes. The lack of connection with his father is not helping Danny feel a sense of connection and security. If the interaction pattern between Danny and his father is changed it may give Danny more access to feeling secure, as well as shifting the focus of Danny's mother as being the only one who can help Danny.)

T: Why do you choose monsters and demons to draw?
D: I don't know. I like them.
T: Cool. How scary are the monsters?
D: Pretty scary. I drew one with blood coming out of its mouth.
T: How much blood?
D: A lot!
T: Cool. How many pictures do you usually draw a day?
D: A couple.
T: Okay. I think it is good to have an artist in the house.

(Focus on Danny's artwork is shifted from the negative reactions of his parents to acknowledging his artistic talents.)

M: The drawings are good but I don't like the subject matter.
F: I don't know why he doesn't draw something else.
T: Yeah. I want to ask about these upset times a little more. You are saying these last close to two hours?
M: Yes. Sometimes a little less but it's close to two hours. I'm really exhausted at the end of the evening after he settles down.
T: So you're working all day?
M: Yes.
T: [To father] And you are working as well?
F: No. I lost my driver's licence for a year and I'm a truck driver so I have been grounded.
T: Oh. So you have to hang around the house?
F: Yeah.
T: What do you do during the day?
F: I just sit around, maybe watch television.
T: It sounds like you are a little bored.
F: Yeah, big time.
T: What time does Danny usually get home from school?

M: He is home by three o'clock.

T: [To father] Since Danny gets home from school around three, what do you guys do together since you are both at home?

F: Not much. He usually stays in his room. Sometimes he may come out and watch television.

(The pattern of limited interaction between Danny and his father is becoming more apparent.)

T: I see. How often were you home when you were driving your truck?

F: I could come home most weekends but I would get into town Saturday morning and have to leave Sunday evening.

T: Oh, so you weren't home too often at all were you?

F: No but I have to make a living.

T: Sure. How long had you been doing this job?

F: I have been driving for close to nine years.

T: Okay. So I want you all to help me by telling me exactly what happens when these upset times happen. I want to understand what each of you is hearing, seeing, and feeling. Imagine that this situation has been filmed and I am going to watch it happen. What is the first thing I would see?

M: Danny starts crying and …

T: Hold on … I don't mean to interrupt but I should have been clearer in my request. Let's start from the time you get home from work.

(When attempting to learn what patterns are in process in a situation it is very important to get as much detail as possible from the clients. This is because even a small detail could be used to create a shift in the pattern. It is not always necessary to have clients make a huge change in how they are behaving in order to create a new way of relating to the problem.)

M: Okay, I come in the door and set my things down. Danny is usually in the living room or he comes out when I get home. I start setting things out for dinner and then he starts crying. He then …

T: He starts crying all of a sudden?

M: Yes. He just starts crying and then he starts freaking out. He will start throwing things and screaming.

T: This is around dinner-time?

M: Yes.

T: Dinner and a show, huh?

[Both mother and father laugh]

T: Okay, what next?

M: Danny will start freaking out and throwing things. He will some-
    times fall on the floor and shake. He is yelling out that he wants to
    die. I usually end up on the floor trying to hold him. He will some-
    times tell me that he sees people in the corner who want to hurt
    him but no one is there. It is very scary to me. It's like he changes
    into something else ...

T: Somebody possessed?

M: It seems like it but I don't think he really is.

T: All right. [To father] Where are you and what are you doing during
    this time?

F: I usually am in the back of the house. I come out to try and cook the
    dinner if I can because she is busy trying to help Danny. After that
    I leave them alone and go to the bedroom.

T: So after you finish in the kitchen you leave and go to the
    bedroom?

F: Yeah, there is really nothing I can do. Sometimes it makes
    matters worse if I stay in the living room. He seems to get more
    agitated.

(Danny's father is hiding from the situation in the hope that it will go
away. With the lack of interaction between him and Danny, it may be
an important shift in the outcome of the problem to get the father more
involved.)

M: The doctor has told us she believes Danny may have early evidence
    of schizophrenia but I don't want to believe that. It makes me crazy
    to think he might have something like that.

T: I understand. [Turning to Danny in a playful tone] Dan the man!
    Give me some information about what is happening with you dur-
    ing these upset times.

D: I get really scared ... and I don't want to live any more.

T: What is making you scared?

D: The people I see that want to hurt me. I just don't want to be alive.
T: What do these people look like?
D: Like demons.
T: Kind of like those drawings of yours, huh?
D: Yes.
T: So when Mum gets home you start having these feelings?
D: Yes.

(Even though Danny has had some episodes at other times and places, it appears the majority of his episodes centre around his mother's presence.)

T: Okay. [To mother] What time do you get home from work?
M: Usually about seven in the evening. I start about seven in the morning.
T: That is a very long day. And you said you worked at a diner.
M: Yes. My feet usually hurt pretty badly when I get home.
T: And I'm sure you're extra tired from having to help Danny every evening.
M: Yes.
T: How are you able to work so hard and yet still be able to focus on Danny? I think it is quite remarkable how you are able to muster all the energy to be able to deal with all of this stuff.
M: It isn't easy but I have to work all these hours until he [referring to husband] can get his licence back.
T: Certainly. I want to go back to the artwork Danny has done. Do you draw anything other than monsters?
D: I don't know.
M: He does draw superheroes sometimes.
T: Okay. Danny, what other things do you do well?

(Danny is quiet, as he doesn't know how to answer the question.)

T: Can't think of anything?

(Danny shakes his head "no")

T: Okay.
F: He can belch really loud.

[All laugh]

T: Really? Seriously you can do that?

[Danny nods "yes"]

T: Can you do it whenever you want?
D: Yeah.
M: He can belch fairly loud. I get on to him at the table when he does it. But he [pointing at her husband] just laughs and tells me to lighten up.
T: Does it bother you a lot that he does that?
M: Not really … as long as he knows not to do it at someone else's house.
T: How loud can you belch? Could you give me a demonstration?

[Danny looks at his mother]

T: I see you checking with Mum but it's okay if you do that in here now. If that is okay with your parents …
M: It's fine if you want him to do it.
T: Sure. I would like to hear how loud he can do it. [To Danny] Go ahead and do it.

[Danny smiles and quickly produces a very loud, deep, and resonate belch.]

T: Wow! That is amazing!

[Mother, father, and Danny laugh]

T: Seriously, that was extraordinary! That did not sound like it came from an eight year old. How did you learn to do that?
D: I don't know … I just do it.
M: I tell him he must have learned it from his father.
T: [To father] Do you have a belch like that?
D: He has a louder burp than me.
T: Is that true?
M: Yep.
F: I may have a loud one now but not when I was as young as Danny.

T: [To mother] Do you also have a good belch?

M: No. I can't do what they do. I don't know if I would want to try.

T: Why not?

M: [laughs] Oh … I guess girls aren't supposed to do that.

T: So you aren't able to join in with these guys, huh?

(By utilising Danny's belching as a resource an opportunity is created to begin building a connection between Danny and his father. Danny's mother states girls are not supposed to belch like boys so this is one area that Danny and his father have in common. They are the "boys" of the house.)

M: No, I don't think so.

T: [To Danny and Father] Have you two ever had a burping contest?

[Danny laughs]

F: [smiling] No.

T: I wonder who would win?

D: Not me!

T: I wouldn't be so sure. You are pretty good at it. I was surprised how loud you got.

F: I think Danny would win.

D: No!

[Both Danny and father laugh]

T: This is really interesting to me. I am going to give you guys a task to do for me. This is a very serious task. It may sound trivial and silly but it is really important, okay?

F: Okay.

T: I need you and Danny to rehearse and practise belching this week so that you can put on a special nightly belching performance for Mum.

D: Huh?

T: Seriously. I want you both to rehearse for five minutes before Mum comes home and as soon as Mum comes in and sets her things down you two are to do a belching performance for maybe a minute.

(This task is given to shift the pattern of lack of interaction between father and son, as well as to change one aspect of what happens when the mother comes home from work.)

M: Why would they do that?

T: I think it is very important for them to show you how well they can get along when you are not home. I can tell that you are a good mother and probably worry about them when you are at work so when you get home you have evidence of how well they are doing and how much fun they are having. This is a crazy assignment, isn't it?

F: It is.

T: [To father] I know you are trying the best you can to make things nice at home for your wife. The fact that you come in and help out in the kitchen when she is busy trying to help Danny shows me how much you care about her. I think this would be a different way to help her relax in knowing you two are all right. I know you probably want your wife to be able to worry less and feel more comfortable when she is at work.

F: Yeah ...

M: I do worry about them.

T: Sure. Now, Mum, you have to grade them on their burping every evening. I think you should give them a number score. You know, like in gymnastics or skating ... like a number on a one to ten scale.

M: Okay. So it is like the higher on the scale, the better they did?

T: Yes. For instance, the belch that Danny did a minute ago might rank as an eight or nine. It would certainly be at least a seven.

M: Okay.

(Having the mother grade the belching contest sets up a new pattern of the two "boys" working together to please the mother. The mother is till a part of the interaction but is not a part of the connection between father and son.)

T: [To Danny and father] Now I want to be clear that this performance is not a competition between you two but rather you are to work together and create a different way of belching every night. You could belch together. You could take turns. You could try to make musical burps. There are a lot of things that the two of you could do to come up with new and interesting ways to show off your belching skills.

F: Seriously? [still in disbelief at the requested task]

T: Yeah, just for one week. Unless you two think you can't belch together. I am sure you two could blow the roof off if you did it together. What do you think Danny?

D: Yeah. It could be loud.

T: How loud?

D: Really loud!

T: I thought so.

M: What if Danny is having an upset episode when I come home?

T: What time does his episode usually start?

M: About seven in the evening.

T: Okay. I think then we either need to have Danny start his episode earlier so that we can still have time for the performance before it gets too late or he can hold off on the episode and do the performance first.

M: What if he isn't feeling upset or if he can't stop himself from having an episode.

T: I think we need to set down the ground rules here. It is important to Danny that we let him know that you are strong enough to help him. This will give him comfort. So you will absolutely need to stand firm and set the schedule in order to let Danny know that you are strong and will help him. I know this idea of the performance may be odd, weird, or just plain crazy but we need to let everyone in the house know that Danny is going to be okay.

(If Mum sees that Danny will be safe when she is at work it will help her relax and be able to deal with any of these future "upset times" more effectively. If Dad can interact with Danny performing creative belching performances it lets him know that Danny is capable of creating something other than just scary pictures and psychotic episodes.)

T: [To Danny] I think having your parents feel better would probably help you relax a little bit wouldn't it?

[Danny is not sure but nods "yes" anyway]

T: Right. I mean maybe I am off here but I thought those things might be important to you.

M: Sure.

T: Okay. So what time do you get home from work?

M: I get home about 6:45 pm.

T: I would like you to come home from work as soon as you can.
     Before you do anything in the kitchen, I would like you to ask
     Danny to have his upset time early. If he usually starts around sev-
     en then starting ten minutes early won't hurt anything.

(The setting of the time frame of when to perform the upset episode is
a paradoxical intervention that puts the mother in a place of power in
regard to Danny's problem. Previously she was a slave to when it happened and was totally helpless as to how long it lasted. Now if Danny
goes ahead and performs the episode on command he has followed his
mother's instructions. If Danny does not have an episode, then there is
a break in the pattern and a night of peace for the household.)

T: [To Danny] If you feel or see those scary things coming on when
     your mother asks you to have your upset time, feel free to let it
     happen. Don't fight it. If you don't feel like you are going to have
     an upset time then go ahead with the belching performance you
     and your father have prepared. I am sure this is something you can
     do for us.

[Danny nods "yes" but seems perplexed by request]

T: Good. Do you have fizzy water at home?

M: Yes.

T: Fizzy water is a great way to help with the belching performance.
     Do you guys think you could teach Mum to belch louder?

D: [laughs] I don't know.

M: I will pass.

T: [To mother] Can you belch on command?

M: No.

T: [To father] Could you teach her to belch loud and on command?

F: I don't know.

M: It's okay, I don't need to know.

T: Well it might be just as well not to have too many belching experts
     in one house. Let the guys handle that sort of thing.

(This again reinforces the interaction between father and son as
something special that Mum is not directly involved in.)

T: Danny, can you feel upset if you are doing a loud burp? I mean, is it hard to focus on the upset things if you do a really loud burp?

D: I don't know.

T: You haven't tried it yet?

D: No.

T: No worries. It would be interesting to find out, wouldn't it?

[Danny shrugs]

M: He gets really scared when he starts seeing things. He also acts like he wants to die. I don't know how to console him. I try really hard …

T: I am really impressed by how much time you take to help your son. There are not a lot of parents who would be able to attempt to comfort their child after working so hard all day. It is obvious to me how much you care about Danny.

M: I really do.

[Mother looks at Danny who beams back at her.]

T: I am glad to see that this family cares so much about each other.

M: We do.

T: I am still a little unsure about what a freak-out upset time looks like. Do you think you guys could act it out for me?

M: Do you mean pretend it is happening?

T: Yeah, do an impromptu performance of it for me. [To Danny] Is that possible for you?

D: I don't know.

T: Do you think you could fake it and show me how it looks when you have an upset time?

D: I don't think so.

M: He probably can only do it when it is really happening. He may not remember what he is doing as he is so upset.

T: You are probably right about that. [To Danny] I wonder if Dad could act it out for us and you tell him whether he is doing it right or not?

F: You want me to do it?

T: Sure, you don't have to go all out but it really gives me an idea of what this looks like. Since I can't be there when this happens …

F: I don't know if I can do it. I feel pretty silly acting like that.

T: Oh, I understand. I don't think it will be too big a deal since it is just us in the office. No one outside will probably even be able to hear what is going on in the room. I know it seems like a weird request but it would help me so much.

M: [To husband] Go on. You can do it.

F: I just feel a little silly.

T: I know. I hate to ask but you are the only one that can help me with this now.

M: Come on. It will be all right.

F: [reluctantly] Okay. I will do what I can.

(The father is apprehensive about performing this action. He has had limited input in the session so this is a way to not only get more interaction from him but also to have Danny observe his own pattern from a third-party perspective. Danny's father starts shaking and saying a lot of nonsensical words. He starts punching his fits on the seat of the chair and finally gets out of the chair and begins rolling on the floor while yelling out that he is scared and wants to die. He then finishes his performance and returns to his seat.)

T: Wow! That was pretty good. I know you weren't crazy about doing it but you did a really good job!

F: [smiling] Thanks.

T: [To Danny] What do you think of what he did? Was it close to what you do?

D: I don't know … kind of …

T: Good. Now I am going to ask you guys for another big favour. I want Dad to repeat his performance and this time I think Danny should play the part of Mum. [To Danny] I want you to act just like Mum does and do the things she does when you are upset. You don't have to do it perfectly, just do the best you can. [To Mom] I want you play the role of Dad. You will say and do what Dad says and does during these upset times. It is very important to see this happen. I want all of you to think of this as a play and you are actors on the stage. Does everyone think you can do this for me?

(At this point it is important to give this family the experience of changing the characters in the emotional play they have been performing. By shifting the roles of the participants, each one gets a different experience of how another party deals with the problem. This may give each person a new resource or perhaps empathy for the person whose pattern they are performing.)

F: Yes.
M: Yeah.

[Danny nods]

T: Great! I want Dad to start this whole thing just as Danny would and take a little while longer doing this performance than you did last time. [To Danny] I want you and Dad to get ready and I will say "Action!" like in the movies.
D: Okay.
T: And ... action!

(The three family members begin their performance. Dad is even more animated this time as he is really allowing himself to be a little louder and more forceful in his portrayal of Danny. Danny attempts to calm his father in his role of being the mother. Danny keeps asking his father about what is happening to him and even tries to hug his father and tell him that everything will be well. Mom is mostly quiet watching the whole performance. As Danny awkwardly attempts to hug his father while the father is flailing, they both begin to laugh.)

T: [playfully] All right you two ... stay in character!

[The father continues to laugh a little.]

T: [To mother] Actors can be so temperamental to work with ...

[Both mother and father laugh. The family finishes their performance.]

T: That was really good. I so appreciate all of you working so hard in here today. I think we have done some really good work. I really want all of you to work together so Danny can begin to feel better.
M: That's what we want.
T: I know. This is why I know I can count on all of you.

M: You can. We will do whatever we have to do.

T: So, this next week we need to have a series of belching performances for Mum. [To Danny] I want you to really go for it. I want you to belch like you are possessed!

D: Okay!

T: [To mother] Now, I am counting on you to keep this whole performance on track by holding Danny to a schedule for when you get home. Remember, if he feels an upset time coming on early then you just let him have it but if he doesn't want to have it then, go ahead with the performance, okay?

M: Sure.

T: [To father] I'm counting on you to help Danny become a better belcher.

F: I will do what I can but I don't know how this will help. I don't see how this will change Danny's situation. I mean the doctor …

(The father is trying to rationalise and think his way out of the problem. Thinking a way out of the problem has not helped in the past. It is important to utilise his beliefs about the therapeutic task of belching performances as an important part of helping Danny get better.)

T: I know it is a crazy idea, isn't it? Sometimes drastic problems can call for drastic measures. I just think there is something so important about doing it. All I am asking is for you to humour me and do this contest for only one week. I know you want to show Danny and your wife that you are committed to helping this family get better and what better way to show them than belching, right?

F: [laughs] I guess …

M: This will be an interesting week.

T: Yes, and I need you to make sure you are fair in your grading of these belching performances. I want you to keep track of the scores for the week and bring them to me next session, okay?

M: Sure.

(Putting the mother in charge of scoring and bringing the scores to the next session increases the likelihood of the father and Danny following through in performing for her.)

T: [To Danny] Don't let me down. I want a good performance for Mum. I want the neighbours to hear what you and your Dad create, okay?
D: Okay.
T: How loud are you going to get?
D: Real loud!

In follow-up sessions the family related how Danny and his father practised burping together for a few minutes a day. Their belching performances for the mother became more and more elaborate every day. Danny had only three upset times the next week instead of the nightly freak-out. Two weeks after that, his parents related he had only two upset times that week. He continued to improve and report fewer instances of experiencing hallucinations. Danny's father was spending more time with Danny before the mother came home from work. In one of Danny's few upset times the first week after the therapy session, his mother asked his father to help Danny during his episode, which he did without hesitation.

Danny's mother became so hopeful after a full month of minimal freak-outs at home that she talked with Danny's psychiatrist about decreasing or eliminating his use of medication. The psychiatrist was shocked to hear Danny was doing so well particularly as a result of the family seeking therapy. The mother's insistence that Danny's medication be re-evaluated provoked the psychiatrist to send a rather nasty letter to me by way of Danny's mother which detailed how nothing I had done had any effect, as it was only the medication that was helping Danny (Danny had been on this medication for over six months with little to no change in his freak-out behaviour). I graciously accepted the angry letter as a badge of honour and a testimonial for creative therapeutic interventions.

REFERENCES

Argast, T. L., Landis, R. E., & Carrell, P. D. (2001). When to use or not use hypnosis according to the Ericksonian tradition. In: B. B. Geary & J. K. Zeig (Eds.), *The Handbook of Ericksonian Psychotherapy* (pp. 66–92). Phoenix AZ: The Milton H. Erickson Foundation Press.

Cade, B., & O'Hanlon, W. H. (1993). *A Brief Guide to Brief Therapy*. New York: Norton.

Campbell, J. (1949). *The Hero with a Thousand Faces*. Princeton, NJ: Princeton University.

Dolan, Y. M. (1985). *A Path with a Heart: Ericksonian Utilization with Resistant and Chronic Clients*. New York: Brunner/Mazel.

Erickson, B. A., Keeney, B. (2006). *Milton H. Erickson, M.D.: An American Healer*. Sedona, AZ: Ringing Rocks.

Erickson, M. H. (1966). The interspersal hypnotic technique for symptom correction and pain control. *American Journal of Clinical Hypnosis, 8*(3): 198–209.

Erickson, M. H., & Rossi, E. (1980). *The Collected Papers of Milton H. Erickson, M.D.* New York: Irvington.

Erickson, M., & Zeig, J. (1980). Symptom Prescription for expanding the psychotic's worldview. In: E. Rossi (Ed.), *Innovative Hypnotherapy (The Collected Papers of Milton H. Erickson on Hypnosis: Volume 4)*. New York: Irvington.

Erickson, M. H., Rossi, E. L., & Rossi, S. K. (1976). *Hypnotic Realities*. New York: Irvington.

Gibney, P. (2012). Reimagining psychotherapy: an interview with Hillary and Bradford Keeney. *Psychotherapy in Australia, 18*(3): 42–51.

Gilligan, S. (2002). *The Legacy of Milton Erickson: Selected Papers of Stephen Gilligan*. Phoenix AZ: Zeig, Tucker & Theisen.

Gordon, D. (1978). *Therapeutic Metaphors: Helping Others Through the Looking Glass*. Cupertino, CA: META Publications.

Gordon, D., & Meyers-Anderson, M. (1981). *Phoenix: Therapeutic Patterns of Milton H. Erickson*. Capitola, CA: Meta Publications.

Haley, J. (1973). *Uncommon Therapy: The Psychiatric Techniques of Milton H. Erickson, M.D.* New York: Norton.

Haley, J. (1984). *Ordeal Therapy: Unusual Ways to Change Behaviour*. San Francisco, CA: Jossey-Bass.

Haley, J. (1993). *Jay Haley on Milton H. Erickson*. Bristol: Brunner/Mazel.

Havens, R. A. (1996). *The Wisdom of Milton H. Erickson: Human Behaviour and Psychotherapy*. New York: Irvington.

Keeney, H., & Keeney, B. (2013). *Creative Therapeutic Technique: Skills for the Art of Bringing Forth Change*. Phoenix, AZ: Zeig, Tucker & Theisen.

Kottler, J. A., & Carlson, J. (2009). *Creative Breakthroughs in Therapy: Tales of Transformation and Astonishment*. Hoboken, NJ: Wiley.

O'Hanlon, B. (1999). *Do One Thing Different: Ten Simple Ways to Change Your Life*. New York: William Morrow.

O'Hanlon, W. H. (1987). *Taproots: Underlying Principles of Milton Erickson's Therapy and Hypnosis*. New York: Norton.

O'Hanlon, W. H., & Hexum, A. L. (1990). *An Uncommon Casebook: The Complete Clinical Work of Milton H. Erickson, M.D.* New York: Norton.

Porges, S. W. (2009). Reciprocal influences between body and brain in the perception and expression of affect: a polyvagal perspective. In: D. Fosha, D. J Siegel & M. Solomon (Eds.), *The Healing Power of Emotion: Affective Neuroscience, Development and Clinical Practice* (pp. 27–54). New York: Norton.

Rosen, S. (1991). *My Voice Will Go With You: The Teaching Tales of Milton H. Erickson*. New York: Norton.

Rossi, E. L. (2002). *The Psychobiology of Gene Expression: Neurogenesis and Neuroscience in Hypnosis and the Healing Arts*. New York: Norton.

Short, D., Erickson, B. A., & Erickson-Klein, R. (2005). *Hope and Resiliency: Understanding the Psychotherapeutic Strategies of Milton H. Erickson, M.D.* Carmarthen: Crown House.

Siegel, D. J. (2012). *Pocket Guide to Interpersonal Neurobiology: An Integrative Handbook of The Mind*. New York: Norton.

Van Der Hart, O. (1983). *Rituals in Psychotherapy: Transition and Continuity.* New York: Irvington.

Watzlawick, P., Weakland, J., & Fisch, R. (1974). *Change: Principles of Problem Formation and Problem Resolution.* New York: Norton.

Zeig, J. K. (1980). *A Teaching Seminar with Milton H. Erickson.* Bristol: Brunner/Mazel.

Zeig, J. K. (1985). *Experiencing Erikson: An Introduction to the Man and His Work.* Bristol: Brunner/Mazel.

Zeig, J. K. & Munion, W. M. (1999). *Milton H. Erickson.* Thousand Oaks, CA: Sage.

INDEX

adrenaline-dumping fear 24
altering patterns, six methods to
    48–57
Alzheimer's disease, stages of 32
anxiety disorder 10
Argast, T. L. 60

Bateson, G. xvii
belching 113–116, 120–121

Cade, B. 40, 47
Campbell, J. 64, 80
Carlson, J. 16
Carrell, P. D. 60
case studies
    African violet queen 12–13
    aggressive child 40
    alcoholic husband 42–43
    alcoholic woman 47
    Antonio 21–22

arguing couples 49–50, 54–56
arguing mother–daughter 52–54
Ariel 67–72
Belinda 84–85
Ben 79–80
boy-who-was-a-dog 33–34
bus-stop woman 32–33
busy street-avoiding man 3
Carol 3–5
Danny 103–121
ditch man 56
Erin 20–21
Evelyn 56–57
flirty woman 31–32
gardening man 77
gardening mother 74
Gary 83–84
Gina 17–19
impotent man 35–36
insecure client 74–75

Jan 6
"Jesus" 32
Joe 72–74
Lily 24–25
Lori 66–67
Miriam 17
money-issues couple 48–49
obsessive man 51
Peggy 37–39
retired police officer 52
schizophrenic son 78
Stanley (the Renaissance man)
    87–102
stroke-survivor 6–7
suicidal woman 29–30
thumb-sucking boy 46
thumb-sucking girl 41
Tom 10–11
Tom (Erickson's) 50
uncreative woman 78
urinating man 46
Walter 81–83
conscious dismissiveness 75

depression 11–13, 17–18, 66, 87–95,
    100, 102
Dolan, Y. M. 27, 60, 75

Erickson, B. A. xiv–xv, 2
Erickson, M. H. xiii–xiv, 59–61, 64,
    75, 77–78
    ability 11
    approach xvi
    assessment 12
    concepts of psychotherapy xiii
    influence xiv
    interventions xvi
    mindset xxi
    perspective 1
    therapy xviii
    way of interacting xv
Erickson-Klein, R. xiv–xv, 2

Gibney, P. 20
Gilligan, S. 27
Gordon, D. 61, 63, 77

Haley, J. xvii–xviii, 2, 7, 41, 78–79
Havens, R. A. 28, 59
hero's journey 64–65
Hexum, A. L. 15, 30

illness 9
impulsive decisions 63
interspersal technique 75
    conscious dismissiveness 75
    unconscious and 75–76
    with stories 75–76

Jung, Carl 19

Keeney, B. xv, 8
Keeney, H. 8
knowledge and ability 61
Kottler, J. A. 16

Landis, R. E. 60

Meyers-Anderson, M. 77
mood disorder 10
Mozart of psychotherapy xvii
multilevel communication
    conscious and unconscious in 60
    interspersal technique 75–76
    therapeutic rituals 80–86
    therapeutic stories 60–75
    therapeutic tasks 77–80
Munion, W. M. 60

Neuro-Linguistic Programming
    (NLP) xviii

O'Hanlon, W. H. xvii, 15, 28, 40, 47,
    45, 61
Oliver, W. 25

paradoxical interventions 40
pattern
    adding to 52–54
    breaking up the 54–56
    changing the duration 48–51
    reversing the 56
Porges, S. W. 10
possessed boy, belched (Danny's
        case study) 103–121
    attempts to calm father 119
    belching by 112–113
    change in behavior 109
    connection with father 113
    father's interaction with 110
    limited interaction with 109, 116
    relationship with parents 107–108
    therapeutic task of belching 120
    upset time 105, 107, 115–116
post-traumatic stress disorder 17
problem land 14
psychological archaeology approach
        23

real alcoholics 42–43
reframing 34–35
    examples of 37–40
Renaissance man (Stanley's case
        study) 87–102
    alcohol problem 93–94
    depression pattern 88–89
    emotional state, examination of 88
    family interaction patterns, shift
        in 91–92
    family team, rebuilding 99
    feeling of significance in 94
    pattern of isolation 94, 99
    physical activity of 94
    role of team 95–96
    verbal agreement for new task 97
resurrection 71–72, 74
Rituals in Psychotherapy: Transition
        and Continuity 81

rituals, therapeutic 80–86
Rosen, S. 52
Rossi, E. L. 10, 35, 51, 75
Rossi, S. K. 75

sensory-based movie 47
Short, D. xiv–xv, 2
shrink games 43
sick person 9, 11, 37
Siegel, D. J. 10
stress eater 79

therapeutic rituals 80–86
    Belinda's case study 84–86
    consciousness shift and 80
    effectiveness of 80–81
    Gary's case study 83–84
    Walter's case study 81–83
therapeutic stories 60–75
    approach 70, 73
    archetypal qualities 74
    Ariel's story 67–72
    call to adventure 68, 73
    Campbell's "hero's journey"
        64–65
    constructing 66–75
    crossing threshold 69, 73
    effectiveness of 62–63
    essential aspect 63
    Goldilocks (children's story
        character) 63–64
    impulsive decisions 63
    interspersal technique with
        75–76
    Joe's story 72–75
    Lori's case study 66–67
    meeting mentor 68–69, 73
    ordeal in 70
    ordinary world 67–68, 72
    positive internal responses 61
    refusal of call 68
    resurrection 71–72, 74

reward in 71, 73
road back 71, 73
self-discipline with finances and
    62
source of 61–62
trials and tests 69–70, 73
therapeutic tasks 77–80

unconscious
    role of 59–60

source of innate wisdom 60
utilisation xxi
    defined 29

Van Der Hart, O. 81

Zeig, J. K. xvi, 5, 28–29, 60